YORK NOTES

General Editors: Professor A.N. Jeffares (*University of Stirling*) & Professor Suheil Bushrui (*American University of Beirut*)

Christopher Marlowe

DOCTOR FAUSTUS

Notes by Christopher Murray

MA (NUI) PHD (YALE)
Lecturer in English Literature,
University College, Dublin

D0544477

LONGMAN
YORK PRESS

YORK PRESS
Immeuble Esseily, Place Riad Solh, Beirut.

LONGMAN GROUP UK LIMITED
Longman House, Burnt Mill, Harlow,
Essex CM20 2JE, England
and Associated Companies throughout the world.

First published 1981
Reprinted 1989

ISBN 0-582-02262-2

Produced by Longman Group (FE) Ltd
Printed in Hong Kong

Contents

Part 1

Introduction

The life and works of Christopher Marlowe

Christopher Marlowe was born in February 1564 in the city of Canterbury, in Kent. His father, John Marlowe, carried on the trade of a shoemaker in Canterbury, while Christopher bettered himself by winning scholarships, first to the King's Grammar School and later (in 1580) to Corpus Christi College in the University of Cambridge. The nature of his university scholarship was such that Marlowe was apparently intended for ordination, but about 1585 he seems to have altered his direction. He commenced study for the MA degree but then absented himself for some time from the university. Strange to relate, he was away on secret service for the government of Queen Elizabeth, and spent some time at the Jesuit seminary at Rheims, in France, perhaps spying upon possible enemies of the Queen, since a conspiracy among Catholics, the Babington Plot, was at this time forming against Elizabeth. The university authorities interpreted Marlowe's absence at Rheims as a serious breach of regulations, and were not inclined to award him the MA degree in 1587, until a letter arrived from the Privy Council signifying his legitimate reason for being away. This letter is evidence of what otherwise would be incredible to us—that a student should actually be employed in the Secret Service. It is a hotly debated question how far Marlowe continued to be involved, for there is no evidence that he was occupied in such activities after he left Cambridge in 1587. But he met his death, as will be seen below, in most mysterious circumstances, and in the company of known activists in the Secret Service. Thus a certain amount of mystery, and more than a whiff of political intrigue, surrounds the short career of Christopher Marlowe.

He is known to us primarily as a poet and playwright, a romantic figure indeed, whose varied works and dazzling originality make him one of the most attractive and most interesting writers in the history of English literature. He began to write while at Cambridge, first making mellifluous translations of the Latin poets Ovid and Lucan and then writing his first play, *Dido, Queen of Carthage* (*c*.1585). Already the choice of topic marks Marlowe as a Renaissance man, a poet in love with the pagan world of ancient Rome. *Dido*, based on the narrative in Virgil's (70–19 BC) *Aeneid*, is rather stiff and stilted, but as it captures the note of romantic ardour so characteristic of the love poetry of the

Elizabethan age it may be called a significant translation of the Latin to the English style. Besides this romantic ardour *Dido* exemplifies Marlowe's early use of blank verse, or iambic pentameter. This verse form, employing a ten-syllable line with alternate unstressed and stressed syllables, made its entry into English literature with the Earl of Surrey's translation of Virgil's *Aeneid* (*c*.1540), and had entered drama with the tragedy *Gorboduc*, by Sackville and Norton, twenty years later. But it was Marlowe who for the first time showed what an instrument blank verse could be, by releasing it from the monotonous regularity of his predecessors and letting the lines flow on with a rhythm that was natural rather than artificial.

The theme of *Dido* was, as Shakespeare's Hamlet remarked, 'caviare to the general', but it 'pleased not the million'. Marlowe's next play, however, launched him as a popular dramatist, the 'angry young man' of his day. The play was *Tamburlaine the Great*, acted at one of the public theatres in London, probably at the end of 1587. It is a breathtaking play in many ways, telling of the rise of the shepherd Tamburlaine to become emperor of the Eastern world, through sheer courage and exercise of will. Here for the first time the typical Marlowe 'voice' is heard, sounding the note of man's yearning for the infinite:

> Nature, that fram'd us of four elements
> Warring within our breasts for regiment,
> Doth teach us all to have aspiring minds:
> Our souls, whose faculties can comprehend
> The wondrous architecture of the world,
> And measure every wandering planet's course,
> Still climbing after knowledge infinite,
> And always moving as the restless spheres,
> Will us to wear ourselves and never rest　　　(II.7.18–26)

Although Tamburlaine is violent and even brutal, his energy makes him admirable, and the admiration he invites is totally new in English literature, for it is amoral. There must have been many indeed who thrilled to the new accent of the Marlovian hero, boasting blasphemously that 'I hold the Fates bound fast in iron chains,/And with my hand turn Fortune's wheel about'. Marlowe quickly wrote a sequel, continuing Tamburlaine's world conquests. Inevitably, there is a falling-off of interest here, because of the repetitive nature of the plot, and it is difficult to see any overall unifying theme in the two parts of *Tamburlaine* taken as a whole.

Marlowe's style of drama seems to have struck a chord in the public consciousness. Although it is not possible to give the precise order in which the rest of his plays were written, it is generally agreed that *Doctor Faustus* came at the end of Marlowe's short career, in 1592 or 1593. In any event, within six years he wrote the seven plays which comprise his total output, which argues an intense, brilliant personality. The variety of the output is equally astonishing, ranging from classical tragedy through the grim and black comedy of *The Jew of Malta* to the history play *Edward II*. All his plays have faults, such as an exaggerated use of violence or a lack of control over the plot, and several were written with the aid of another hand or hands, but they all demonstrate a fitful brilliance. Only in the area of comedy was Marlowe deficient; in all other areas he paved the way for England's greatest dramatist, William Shakespeare, born in the same year as Marlowe.

Some would say, indeed, that Marlowe was Shakespeare's rival in love as well as in composition, for they identify as Marlowe the rival poet in Shakespeare's sonnets to his Dark Lady. But such identification is without substance. So far as is known, there was no contact between Shakespeare and Marlowe, although Shakespeare plainly knew Marlowe's plays well enough to quote from them on occasion.

In London, Marlowe moved among a circle of writers known as the 'University Wits', graduates of Oxford and Cambridge. This circle included Robert Greene (1558–92), Thomas Nashe (1567–1601) and George Peele (1557–98), playwrights and prose-writers of some distinction. It was a bohemian life they led, for playwriting was not then a respectable profession, and Marlowe, like so many of his contemporaries, was at times in trouble with the law. In 1589, for example, he was charged along with another man for the murder of one William Bradley; Marlowe was found not guilty, and appears only to have been witness to the incident, but somehow he acquired the reputation none the less of being a hotheaded, violent man. Again, the contrast with 'gentle' Shakespeare is often made. But we really have not enough reliable evidence to brand Marlow as a habitually violent man, unless, of course, we take the coroner's report at the inquest into Marlowe's death as absolutely true, which would be unwise. According to this report, on 30 May 1593 Marlowe spent the day at the house of a widow, Eleanor Bull, at Deptford Strand, just outside London, in the company of three men. What the purpose of the day-long meeting was is not stated, but the four men dined and then quarrelled over the 'reckoning' (the bill). Marlowe is said to have grabbed the dagger of one of the men, Ingram Frizer, and stabbed him twice in the head; Frizer struggled for possession of his knife and in the struggle drove its point into Marlowe's skull and killed him instantly. Frizer was found innocent and granted a Queen's pardon. There are too many questions surrounding the circumstances of Marlowe's death to allow its acceptance as the wages of sin.

Two quite distinct areas deserve comment in this regard. Firstly, all three of the men with whom Marlowe spent his last day were Secret

Service men, and one of them, Robert Poley, had been prominent in disclosing the Babington Plot against Queen Elizabeth in 1586. Marlowe had had experience in Sir Francis Walsingham's Secret Service himself (in 1587); it is within the bounds of possibility that he had become a danger and was assassinated. On the other hand, an assassination could surely have been arranged with less trouble and in less suspicious circumstances than is the case here. We simply do not know enough to be sure that the death of Marlowe was political. Moreover, the question hardly concerns Marlowe as playwright.

The other question strikes at the heart of Marlowe's drama, since it is a question of belief. On the day before Marlowe's death a detailed report was delivered to the Privy Council, accusing him of atheism, blasphemy and homosexuality, any one of which charges would have been enough to have Marlowe condemned to death. Indeed, the man who drew up the report, Richard Baines, an informer, expressed the view that 'the mouth of so dangerous a member may be stopped'. In other words, Baines recommended the elimination of Marlowe. The list of his charges is considerable, but atheism is the basic and recurring accusation. Can it be mere coincidence that Baines's report (and recommendation) reached the Privy Council just at the time when Marlowe actually met his death? When Baines put the wrong date on his report (2 June) and then claimed that Marlowe died three days later we are entitled to be suspicious.

That Marlowe should have been accused of atheism may surprise readers of *Doctor Faustus*, in which Christian doctrine underpins the tragedy firmly. But by 'atheism' the Elizabethans meant what we might call 'free thinking', meaning an intellectual probing of established doctrine. During the later 1580s there was an active group of intellectuals in London, known as the School of Night, who debated matters of science and belief and, it seems, came down in favour of 'atheistic' attitudes. Sir Walter Ralegh (1552–1618) was a prominent member, as was the mathematician Thomas Harriot (1560–1621), and for a time Giordano Bruno (1548–1600) presided at the London meetings. In 1594 charges of atheism were brought against the members of the School of Night. Since Marlowe was a member, his accusation was clearly preliminary to a general purge. One of Marlowe's associates, Robert Greene, warned him from his deathbed against atheism, and especially against the ideas of Niccolò Machiavelli (1469–1527), the Italian statesman and author of the political treatise *Il Principe* [*The Prince*] (1532):

> Why should thy excellent wit, his [God's] gift, be so blinded, that thou shouldst give no glory to the giver: Is it pestilent Machiavellian policy that thou hast studied? O peevish folly! What are his rules but mere confused mockeries, able to extirpate in small time the generation of mankind? .... Wilt thou my friend be his disciple? Look

but to me, by him persuaded to that liberty, and thou shalt find it an infernal bondage.

Another friend, Thomas Kyd (1558–94), became so frightened when he was arrested in May 1593 (three weeks before Marlowe's death) that he immediately accused his friend in order to save his own skin. Among Kyd's papers at the time of his arrest was found an atheistic essay, and he insisted that it belonged to Marlowe, whose room-mate he had been two years earlier. Under torture he confessed much more, and it is surprising how his accusations against Marlowe happen to tally with what the informer Baines wrote in his report to the Privy Council.

It may be concluded, then, that Marlowe was an intellectual, an arrogant sceptic who delighted in making fun of sacred things, and that his outspoken comments on the Bible and on certain points of Christian doctrine shocked and alarmed some of his contemporaries. We may speculate that in the last decade of Queen Elizabeth's reign the authorities regarded with suspicion any and every departure from orthodoxy, since, as Elizabeth had no obvious heir, a rebellion, or a coup, was a constant fear. And we may reasonably imagine that Marlowe fell foul of the authorities in such circumstances, because of his fearless and perhaps ill-advised expressions of 'atheism'. What is beyond dispute is that he was cut off in his prime, at the age of twenty-nine, in a tragic manner. It is a supreme irony that one of the last of his creations was Doctor Faustus, the 'atheist' who is overtaken by a violent end. But we must resist the temptation to see Doctor Faustus as a self-portrait.

The text of *Doctor Faustus* and its problems

The age and the play

As a preliminary to a discussion of the textual problems surrounding *Doctor Faustus* it may be pointed out that in general plays during the Elizabethan period rated very low on the scale of books published. Plays were regarded as ephemeral, since there were new plays almost every day at the public theatres, and publication was exceptional rather than the rule.

Publication of plays usually occurred as a means of securing title, or what, today, we call copyright. If a company of actors had a success with a new play it sometimes happened that a 'pirate' edition appeared, that is, a version compiled by others without the authority of the playwright. It would be a cheap publication and would probably sell well, and could provide rival companies of actors with a text which they could appropriate for staging. To forestall such a procedure, a company could, for a slight fee, enter the title of a play in the Stationers' Register, naming the publisher, which implied future publication and gave the author protection against 'pirates'. The play itself might not be published for several years, if at all. Marlowe's *The Jew of Malta* was so entered in the Stationers' Register on 17 May 1594 (two years after it was first staged), but the earliest extant edition dates from 1633. Likewise, *Doctor Faustus* was entered in the Stationers' Register on 7 January 1601, and the earliest edition dates from 1604. Although Marlowe was dead in both instances, this move preserved his plays for the Admiral's Men, the company of actors for whom he wrote. But it is obvious that such a procedure implies that the text published might not represent the entire text of the author: one of the basic problems faced by a modern editor is to decide how 'authoritative' the first edition of an Elizabethan play may be.

A play—usually one which had a popular success—was normally published in a Quarto edition, that is, printed on paper one quarter of a sheet in size. A bigger book, such as the collected edition of Shakespeare's thirty-six plays, was printed on folio paper, which is half a sheet. Editions of plays are thus usually referred to as First Quarto, Second Quarto, and so on, meaning the first edition, second edition, and so on. There are usually discrepancies between one edition and the next, and the editor has to try to sift these so as to arrive—ideally—at what the author actually wrote in the first place.

Dating and source

We have often, then, to work backwards from the first Quarto to establish probable date of composition. External and internal evidence are used further to decide the date. External evidence would include date of staging, or references to the play in contemporary records such as Philip Henslowe's (*d*.1616) diary. In the 1590s Henslowe operated the Rose Theatre in London (where *Doctor Faustus* was staged), and kept records of payments to actors and playwrights, as well as records of performances; accordingly, Henslowe's diary, which has survived, is a most informative source of external evidence for Elizabethan drama of the 1590s. It has been edited in modern times. Internal evidence can be a matter of allusion by the author or a matter of stylistic usages. Where an author makes a topical reference, this can aid the dating but sometimes a topical reference has to be received with caution. In *Doctor Faustus*, for instance, there is a reference to Dr Lopez (IV.5.48), who was private physician to Queen Elizabeth and was accused of having entered into a plot to poison her; he was put on trial in February 1594 and executed in June. This was a year after Marlowe's own death. Since the reference is in the past tense it is clear that Marlowe cannot have written this passage—it is the mark of another hand in the play.

Stylistic usages, especially use of verse patterns, can suggest a likely date of composition, but this kind of evidence requires very careful handling, and must be backed up by stringent, objective criteria. It is usually used to corroborate other evidence.

Doctor Faustus was based on a German narrative, describing the career of an actual academic who sold his soul to the devil. This narrative was published in German in 1587, but an English translation did not appear until a few years later. The sole surviving copy of *The Historie of the Damnable Life, and Deserved Death of Doctor John Faustus* is in the British Library, London. It was published in 1592. It is beyond dispute that Marlowe used this *Historie* for his play, which means that he wrote *Doctor Faustus* in the last year of his short life. As the source describes such comic incidents as the Horse-courser's experience with the horse bought from Faustus, and the 'horning' of the knight at the Emperor's court, we must believe that such scenes formed part of the whole design of the play, even though it is commonly accepted (from internal evidence) that Marlowe did not himself write the comic scenes in the play.

A note on the text

The first extant edition of *Doctor Faustus*, the first Quarto, dates from 1604, eleven years after Marlowe's death. This Quarto shows the hand of an unknown collaborator. It is known as the A-text, in order to distinguish it from the substantially different version of the play which was printed in 1616, known as the B-text. The latter contains 2121 lines, as against 1517 lines in the A-text.

For a long time, scholars inclined to the belief that the A-text was more authoritative, closer to what Marlowe intended. But modern scholars have shown that the opposite is the case. The main piece of evidence is the existence of an anonymous play printed in 1594, entitled *The Taming of A Shrew* (not to be confused with Shakespeare's comedy), in which several passages echo passages from *Doctor Faustus*, and in each case the echo is traceable to the B-text rather than the A-text. The latter is now thought to have been a reconstruction made from memory by various persons, who included at least one actor in the original production of about 1592–3. Thus, the 1604 text is regarded as a 'bad' Quarto.

A complication in the matter of the authenticity of the B-text arises when we find in Henslowe's diary an entry, dated 22 November 1602, recording the payment of four pounds to two hack writers for their 'additions' to *Doctor Faustus*. Some scholars argue that these additions—which must have been considerable, since six pounds was Henslowe's payment for a full new play—are now lost, and are, accordingly, not in the B-text at all. But the editor of a recent edition of

Marlowe's works published by the Cambridge University Press (see Part 5), Professor Fredson Bowers, argues that the additions are to be found mainly in Act IV of the B-text. He also holds that the two hack writers, William Birde and Samuel Rowley, revised some earlier scenes in the play. Bowers still admits the work of Marlowe's original collaborator, whoever he was, which Birde and Rowley either let stand or else touched up—virtually all of this material is in the comic or farcial episodes. Apart from the Choruses, Bowers ascribes only eight out of the total nineteen scenes to Marlowe; or, including the Choruses, no more than 958 lines out of the total 2121.

All modern editions make the B-text of 1616 the basis of *Doctor Faustus*, in spite of the matter of additions. Therefore any edition that relies mainly on the A-text of 1604 must now be regarded as inadequate. Most modern editions supply the variant readings from the A-text; that is, they include in notes or an appendix the passages that are different. The Penguin edition by J. B. Steane goes a step further and incorporates the A-text into the B-text at occasional points (which he marks carefully in the notes), and the result is an excellent arrangement. Since Professor Steane modernises the spelling and arranges the scenes into acts, his edition is the most satisfactory to handle. Consequently, this edition of Christopher Marlowe, *The Complete Plays*, Penguin Books, Harmondsworth, 1969, is used throughout these notes.

Part 2

Summaries
of DOCTOR FAUSTUS

A general summary

Doctor Faustus tells the story of a scholar at the University of Wittenberg in the sixteenth century, who is so ambitious for fame, power and pleasure that he abandons the legitimate pursuits of academic scholarship in favour of necromancy, or black magic. He conjures up from hell the demon Mephostophilis, and enters into a contract with Lucifer, prince of hell, whereby Faustus may have his heart's desire (with Mephostophilis as his servant) for twenty-four years, at the end of which time his soul must become the possession of Lucifer. Because he disbelieves in hell and its pains, Faustus eagerly enters into this contract, even though he is given grim signs that he is making a deadly mistake. Once this bond is sealed, however, he alternates between a consciousness that he will be eternally damned and a reckless indifference, which permits him to feed his appetite for knowledge, beauty and power.

Faustus travels through the world and even into outer space in company with Mephostophilis, exploring the frontiers of human knowledge, before he descends upon Rome and makes a mockery of the Pope's victory ceremonies, celebrating the defeat of the anti-Pope Bruno. Faustus frees Bruno and flies with him to the court of the Emperor Charles, where he displays his magical powers. After dealing with Benvolio, a knight who mocked him, Faustus travels to the court of the Duke of Vanholt, where he again displays his magical powers, and outwits some would-be comic exploiters. These adventures over, Faustus returns to Wittenberg, where he is received by his friends. He summons up the spirit of Helen of Troy for their admiration, and she becomes his demon lover. He is now assailed by the voices of the Good Angel and the Evil Angel, who renew their exhortations to repentance and despair respectively, just as they had urged at the beginning of Faustus's career as a magician. An Old Man, not seen before, also enters at this point and urges Faustus to repent and change his ways, but he resists, held to his contract by Mephostophilis.

Time is now running out, the twenty-four years are almost spent, and Faustus bids his friends goodbye in a moving scene. Then he faces his last hour alone, meditating in anguish on his dilemma: his yearning, now that he is aware of eternity, to be released from his inevitable damnation, and his simultaneous conviction that it is impossible for him now to repent and be saved. As the clock strikes twelve, the devils come for him and he is carried off to hell. His friends find his mutilated body next morning. A commentator, called the Chorus, who appeared at the beginning of the play to introduce Faustus, sums up by indicating that the fate of Faustus should be an example to all.

Detailed summaries

Preliminary note: As it is here assumed that the reader of these notes is in possession of a modern text of *Doctor Faustus*, preferably the Penguin edition in *Christopher Marlowe: The Complete Plays*, edited by J. B. Steane, which is the edition used here, time will not be wasted in providing notes and explanations readily available. The aim is to provide a linked commentary which may serve to send the reader back to the text with both a stimulated interest and a clearer understanding of what is going on. It need hardly be said that this commentary is no substitute for Marlowe's text. To gain from the commentary, it is best to have read *Doctor Faustus* first, and then to keep the text close by for reference.

Chorus

This is not a chorus in the classical sense, but a speaker of a prologue. This figure also enters twice in the course of the play, filling in information required for the plot, and appears again at the end to deliver a moral summary, very much in the manner of the Doctor at the end of a medieval morality play. Marlowe shows an awareness of the constraints imposed on narrative by the stage, with regard to time and space, and he uses the Chorus to maintain a flow of narrative, which is a selection of crucial moments in Faustus's history. Also, the Chorus speaks with authority, guiding the reader's attitude towards Faustus. He says that Faustus is swollen with 'self-conceit' and pride, and compares him to Icarus, a common Elizabethan reference wherever excessive ambition was being described. The Chorus obviously gestures towards Faustus as he speaks his closing line, 'And this the man that in his study sits'. The scene that follows can thus be interpreted as an illustration of the Chorus's description of Faustus, and the play as a whole may be seen as a more detailed extension of the consequences of the pride here given as the clue to Faustus's fall.

NOTES AND GLOSSARY:

Not marching in the fields of Thrasimene . . .: Marlowe indicates that his play is not a military one, concerned with Roman history (Lake Thrasimene was the place where

Hannibal won a major battle over the Romans in 217 BC), nor is it about love or politics. These opening lines may refer either to Marlowe's ealier plays or to other plays performed by the company of players for whom he wrote

Mars:	Roman god of war
mate:	ally with
Carthigens:	the Carthaginians, inhabitants of the city-state of Carthage, in North Africa, over whom Hannibal (247–*c*.182 BC), the great general, held sway
dalliance:	playfulness
muse:	poet
gentles:	gentlemen
graced:	honoured
swollen . . . self-conceit:	puffed up with a false idea of his own intellectual attainments
waxen wings:	the reference is to Icarus, in Greek mythology, who flew too close to the sun so that it melted the wax attaching the artificial wings to his body and he fell into the sea and was drowned
surfeits:	feeds over-indulgently
necromancy:	black magic

Act I Scene 1

Here we find Faustus in soliloquy, that is, using the convention then accepted on the Elizabethan stage of voicing his secret thoughts aloud. He addresses himself in the third person, saying 'Faustus' where we would expect 'I', and this is a sign of his ability to render his inner self objectively and view it dispassionately. Marlowe in this way attempts to show from the beginning that there are two sides to Faustus, the objective and the subjective, in tension and soon to be in opposition. This depiction of inner conflict was among Marlowe's great contributions to the development of English tragedy. Shakespeare was to refine it and make it more realistic, so that when Hamlet or Macbeth is in soliloquy we hear only the 'I' speaking and we are drawn *within* the mind to share the conflict. As yet, Marlowe depicts the conflict more simply, and, we may feel, more awkwardly.

Faustus is at a crisis point in his life, and is about to turn away completely from all legitimate scholarship. It is a momentous occasion, and we are given a succession of rejections on Faustus's part—of philosophy, of medicine, of law—leading up to the climax, his rejection of divinity, the study of the sacred subject of theology. Marlowe often uses a series in this way. At first it may appear that he is repeating himself, but always there is the effect of steps in a ladder, up to a significant moment of suspense. We see this at large in the whole plot of *Tamburlaine*, which at first seems only an endless succession of fights and victories; but if we look more closely we see that there is an order in the episodes, leading to the marriage of Tamburlaine to Zenocrate. Likewise, in the episodes of *Doctor Faustus* there is a cumulative progression towards the scene at the Duke of Vanholt's palace in Act IV, where Faustus stands master of all he surveys, and he then returns home. Thus the opening soliloquy, apart from showing us how arrogantly Faustus rejects orthodox fields of study, indicates how Marlowe organises dramatic action: by episodes that repeat the structure with a cumulative effect, up to some turning-point.

The turning-point here, of course, comes in his welcome to 'necromantic books', the forbidden fruit, as it were, on the Tree of Knowledge. It is significant that the language he uses suddenly becomes excited, enthused, emotional, as indicated by the interjection 'Oh' at line 52, and by the build-up, the cumulation of possessions listed and linked by repetition of 'of':

> Oh, what a world of profit and delight,
> Of power, of honour, of omnipotence,
> Is promised to the studious artizan!

What distinguishes Faustus here is his subjectivity, allied to aspiration. This is the Renaissance aspect of his character, the stress on the individual, in contrast to the conformity, the subordination of self to one's place in the general hierarchy, which distinguished the older, feudal arrangement. It must be accepted that Marlowe makes Faustus attractive as a 'modern' figure, breaking free from the shackles of a limiting social structure. The attractiveness comes through in the energy of Faustus's language, lines 52–62. Can you find the details that suggest this energy?

Wagner, Faustus's servant, enters briefly and is sent to fetch Valdes and Cornelius. Meantime the Good and Evil Angels enter and briefly exhort Faustus. The Evil Angel's last words urge, 'Be thou on earth as Jove is in the sky,' and this appeals greatly to Faustus, as it expresses his ambition precisely. Like Tamburlaine, he wants infinite power. The Angels are projections of the two sides of Faustus's personality, his will to conform and his will to transcend.

Valdes and Cornelius are friends, probably older than Faustus—he refers to their 'sage conference' (line 98), or wise advice. They serve to spur on Faustus's ambitions, and they provide him with information on how to conjure spirits, but they play no further role in the plot. In terms of dramaturgy, or the craft of playwriting, this sudden introduction and abandoning of functional characters may be considered a fault.

Marlowe seems careless about everything except the basic situation of his hero, Faustus, who is about to make a terrifying leap into the dark.

Having listened eagerly to their urgings, Faustus invites Valdes and Cornelius to dine with him, after which Valdes is to instruct him 'in the rudiments' of black magic, and then Faustus will go to 'some solitary grove' with certain books, and 'try his cunning by himself', that is, attempt to raise spirits.

NOTES AND GLOSSARY:

Analytics: logic. Also the name given to two works by Aristotle (384–322BC), the Greek philosopher, on the nature of proof in argument. In the opening part of his soliloquy, Faustus makes several references to the traditional scholastic syllabus, or university curriculum. Marlowe takes care to translate many of the Latin and Greek quotations in the text itself

Galen: Greek physician (AD130–200) and author, the leading authority on medicine in the Middle Ages

ubi desinit philosophus, ibi incipit medicus: *(Latin)* 'where the philosopher leaves off, the doctor begins' (Aristotle)

Justinian: Justinian I (ADc.482–565), the Roman Emperor who codified the law, in the *Institutiones* referred to and quoted from in this passage

Si una eademque res legatur duobus,/Alter rem, alter valorem rei: *(Latin)* a quotation from Justinian: 'If one and the same thing is bequeathed to two persons, one of them shall have the thing, the other the value of the thing'

Exhaereditare filium non potest pater, nisi—: *(Latin)* Another quotation from Justinian: 'The father may not disinherit the son, except—'

Jerome's Bible: the Vulgate or Latin Bible translated by Saint Jerome in AD405. The sentences which Faustus quotes and translates are from Romans VI:23 and 1 John I:8

artizan: artisan, craftsman; here, 'practitioner of magic'

conference: conversation

Jove: God

conceit: the idea

Resolve me: free me (from doubt)

I'll have them wall all Germany with brass: the English scholar-alchemist Roger Bacon (c.1214–94) planned to wall England thus. See also Robert Greene's play, *Friar Bacon and Friar Bungay* (1594)

Prince of Parma:	the Spanish governor of the Netherlands (from 1572 to 1592) and enemy of England
fiery keel:	a fireship that destroyed the bridge built by the Prince of Parma over the river Scheldt
gravell'd:	brought to a stop, baffled
Musaeus:	legendary pre-Homeric Greek poet
Agrippa:	Cornelius Agrippa (1485–1535), humanist and reputed magician
Almain rutters:	German cavalry-men
golden fleece:	sought by Jason, in Greek mythology. Marlowe is here also referring to the treasure fleets of King Philip II (1527–98) of Spain

Enrich'd with tongues: skilled in languages

Bacon's and Albanus' works: the works of Roger Bacon (referred to above), and Pietro d'Abano (c.1250–1316), Italian philosopher and supposed sorcerer

Hebrew Psalter:	the Psalms in the Old Testament of the Bible. Certain psalms and the opening words of St John's gospel were used in conjuring spirits

canvass every quiddity: discuss every detail

Act I Scene 2

Two Scholars wonder what has become of Faustus, who used to be so prominent in scholastic debates. Wagner, foolishly using the language of such debates, informs them that Faustus is at dinner with Valdes and Cornelius. This news prompts the First Scholar to fear that Faustus has fallen 'into the damned art' for which Valdes and Cornelius are 'infamous through the world'. The Second Scholar echoes this concern, which thus provides a note of foreboding in the tragedy.

NOTES AND GLOSSARY:

sic probo:	*(Latin)* 'Thus I prove it'. A term used in scholastic argument
presently:	immediately
corpus naturale ... mobile: (Latin)	'a natural body and thus capable of movement'. Wagner provides a scrap from Aristotle on physics
licentiates:	qualified to go on to a master's degree, or doctor's degree
stand:	rely

the place of execution: here, the dining-room

a precisian:	a Puritan
Rector:	head of the university

Act I Scene 3

Faustus, apparently at the 'solitary grove' mentioned above, begins to conjure up devils. The scene begins, however, with a stage direction: *'Thunder. Enter* LUCIFER *and* FOUR DEVILS', and Faustus speaks *'to them with this speech'*. This is pure theatre, in the sense that atmosphere is given priority. The awesomeness of what Faustus is about to do was communicated to the Elizabethan audience by the appearance, *in advance*, of the devils on stage, while the thunder signified disorder in nature and thus evil.

Faustus does some 'business', that is, he makes a circle and apparently uses his books, before calling in Latin for the blessing of the gods of the underworld and the rising of Mephostophilis. In the middle of his conjuration occurs the world 'Dragon', apparently the prompter's cue to have the dragon-costumed devil ready; when this devil enters (line 22) Faustus sardonically bids him go and return as 'an old Franciscan friar', which would be more like a devil. This is an anti-Catholic reference, seen far more strongly in the scenes where the Pope appears (Act III). Marlowe's play was intended, of course, for the largely Protestant audiences of Reformation England.

Mephostophilis enters when Faustus commands again, and tells him that devils always come when they see a soul 'in danger to be damned'. Faustus's pride is seen in his failure to take warning from Mephostophilis' words. Also, he questions Mephostophilis flippantly about hell. It is ironic that all through this scene Lucifer and the four devils are also present: Faustus chooses to ignore them because he disbelieves in the idea of 'damnation'. He is unmoved by Mephostophilis' plangent cry that hell is everywhere that God is not: the mocking Faustus we see here alerts us to the real danger he is in and ignores. He sends Mephostophilis off to tell Lucifer of his wish to trade his soul for twenty-four years of 'all voluptuousness' and power. He makes an appointment to hear Mephostophilis' reply at midnight in his study. Alone, he muses on the power he will soon possess.

In what way does this scene, and in particular Faustus's last speech (lines 102–14) modify the earlier view we might have of Faustus as admirably daring?

NOTES AND GLOSSARY:
Orion's drizzling look: the constellation Orion was traditionally associated with rain
From th'Antarctick world: Marlowe, seemingly, thought that the night comes on from the south (instead of the west)
welkin: sky
anagrammatised: the spelling rearranged to make other words

characters:	marks, or seals, believed to derive from stellar rays. Magicians who could reproduce these 'characters' could make use of the power exerted by the stars
Sint mihi dei acherontis . . .: (Latin)	'May the gods of the underworld be kind to me; may the triple deity of Jehovah [God] be gone; greetings to the spirits of fire, air and water. Prince of the east [Lucifer], Belzebub monarch of the fires below, and Demogorgon, we ask your favour so that Mephostophilis may appear and rise. Why do you delay? By Jehovah, hell and the holy water which now I sprinkle, and the sign of the cross which now I make, and by our prayers let Mephostophilis himself now rise, compelled to serve us'
Quin redis Mephostophilis fratris imagine? (Latin)	'Why do you not return, Mephostophilis, in the appearance of a friar?'
rack [verb]:	torment (by anagrammatising, in this case)
confound hell in elysium:	Faustus does not distinguish between hell and the pagan afterworld

---

Act I Scene 4

(Written not by Marlowe but by his unknown collaborator.) Wagner, Faustus's servant, asks the Clown if he will be 'my man and wait on me'. In the comic business which follows, two devils chase the Clown up and down, and he agrees to serve Wagner.

NOTES AND GLOSSARY:

comings in:	income
goings out:	expenditure
Qui mihi discipulus: (Latin)	'One who is my pupil'. The opening words of a poem used in Elizabethan schools
stavesacre:	flea powder
familiars:	spirits or devils attendant on a human being
guilders:	Dutch money. Here, hiring money
pressed:	drafted
Quasi vestigias nostras insistere: (Latin)	'as if to tread in our footsteps'
plackets:	petticoats
fustian:	bombast, excessive wordiness

Act I Scene 5

(This is Act II Scene 1 in some modern editions.) Faustus in his study, apparently waiting for Mephostophilis's reply from Lucifer, soliloquises on his probable damnation. He wavers between a desire to turn to God again and despair. The Good and Evil Angels enter again and press these same contraries. Again, the last words of the Evil Angel revive Faustus's ambition, and then Mephostophilis enters. Faustus must make a formal contract with Lucifer, signing it with his blood. But quite dramatically Faustus's blood congeals as he is signing his name and he is left alone while Mephostophilis goes to fetch coals to dissolve it. 'What might the staying of my blood portend?' Faustus muses, and impresses on the audience the terrible significance of the act he is undertaking. A moment of 'arrest', of pause, like this is always effective in tragedy. It serves to underline the moral meaning of the choice being made.

After Mephostophilis re-enters, and Faustus finishes his signature, he is given a second sign: the words *'Homo fuge!'* or 'Fly, O man!' Mephostophilis puts on a dance of devils, who give crowns and rich costumes to Faustus, as if to pledge his imperial greatness. After this piece of spectacle the contract is read in all its conditions, and Faustus says he is satisfied. He then questions Mephostophilis again about hell, and again his arrogance is evidenced in his insistence that 'hell's a fable', in spite of Mephostophilis' evidence to the contrary. A comic note is introduced when Faustus asks for a wife, and is granted a devil *'with fireworks'* which he hastily rejects and accepts instead the conjuring book which will bring him all the pleasures and all the knowledge he desires.

NOTES AND GLOSSARY:

what boots it?:	what does it matter?
Abjure:	forswear
Signory of Emden:	Governorship of a large north-west German port which traded with England
veni, veni, Mephostophile!:	*(Latin)* 'come, come, Mephostophilis!'
Solamen miseris, socios habuisse doloris:	*(Latin)* 'It is a consolation to the wretched to have had companions in woe'
proper:	own
streams:	this word is used of Christ's blood in the final scene, thereby linking Faustus's guilt with its retribution
Consummatum est:	*(Latin)* 'It is finished'. These were the last words of Jesus Christ on the cross. Faustus's use of them is blasphemous
Homo fuge!:	*(Latin)* 'Fly, O man!'
Penelope:	The faithful wife of Ulysses in Homer's epic poem, the *Odyssey*
Saba:	the Queen of Sheba, in the Bible, 1 Kings 10
chafer:	grate
one self place:	one and the same place
fond:	foolish
iterating:	repeating

harness:	armour
dispositions:	situations (astrological)

Act II Scene 1

Faustus in his study muses, 'When I behold the heavens then I repent.'
Mephostophilis reminds Faustus that loss of heaven's joys was of his own
seeking. The Good Angel and the Evil Angel briefly urge and discourage
repentance, but Faustus considers his heart 'so hardened that I cannot
repent'.

That considerable time has now passed is indicated by Faustus's
admission that he would have committed suicide 'long ere this' had not
'sweet pleasure conquered deep despair'. When he reflects upon one of
those pleasures, given by Homer and Amphion, he resolves not to repent,
and turns instead to disputing cosmology with Mephostophilis. The latter
outlines the theory of Ptolemy, which was still the concept of the cosmos
believed by Marlowe's contemporaries. (It was soon to be disproved by
Galileo.) But when Mephostophilis refuses to answer the question, 'who
made the world?', and exits, Faustus falls back into despair. The Good
and Evil Angels reappear very briefly, drawing a prayer from Faustus,
which leads to the immediate arrival of Lucifer and Belzebub from hell, to
rebuke him. Faustus 'repents' of his lapse—we may be expected here to
see that he is in a double bind between God and Lucifer.

Belzebub announces a 'pastime', a pageant of the Seven Deadly Sins.
There follows a section in prose (lines 103–90, at the end of the scene),
which may not have been written by Marlowe. (The names of Thomas
Nashe and Samuel Rowley (*c*.1585–*c*.1625) have both been suggested as
the possible collaborator here.) Faustus is pleased by the pageant and
Lucifer promises to come at midnight to show him the delights of hell. He
leaves Faustus a book by which to transform himself into whatever shape
he please.

NOTES AND GLOSSARY:

buzzeth:	mutters
Alexander:	Paris of Troy, who loved Oenone but deserted her for Helen, in Homer's *Iliad*
He, that built the walls of Thebes:	Amphion, who with his harp made the stones move so as to form the walls of Thebes (in Greek mythology)
astrology:	astronomy applied to human uses
This centric earth:	Marlowe conceives of the universe with the earth as centre and the moon and other 'planets' moving in eight 'spheres' or orbits around it (the succeeding passage explains this Ptolemaic system)

termine: extremity

situ et tempore: *(Latin)* 'in position and in time', that is, in direction of movement and in revolution around the earth

poles of the zodiac: common axle on which all the spheres revolve

freshmen's suppositions: elementary assumptions, as taught to first-year students

intelligentia: *(Latin)* spirit. It was said that an angel controlled the motion of a planet within its 'sphere' or orbit

coelum igneum et cristallinum: *(Latin)* 'fiery and crystalline sphere' beyond God's empyrium

conjunctions: apparent proximity of heavenly bodies

oppositions: an extreme apparent divergence of heavenly bodies

aspects: the relative positions of heavenly bodies

Per inequalem motum, respectu totius: *(Latin)* 'On account of their unequal motion with respect to the whole'. That is, the heavenly bodies move at different speeds

dam: wife

gratify: reward

Ovid's flea: In a medieval poem, 'Elegy for a Flea', wrongly attributed to the Latin poet Ovid (43BC–AD18), the lover envies the flea's free access to the lady's body

cloth of Arras: rich tapestry, from Arras in northern France

Begotten of a chimney-sweeper and an oyster-wife: consequently, dirty and smelly

case: pair

bevers: snacks

mutton: here, penis

stockfish: codfish

chary: carefully

several: different

Act II Scene 2

(A comic scene, probably not by Marlowe but by his unknown collaborator. It was revised by William Birde (*d.*1624) and Samuel Rowley in 1602.) It concerns Robin the Clown, who has one of Faustus's conjuring books, with which he tries to impress Dick, the ostler, by promising him lots of free wine at the tavern.

NOTES AND GLOSSARY:

as 't passes: as beats everything

A per se ...: *(Latin)* Robin is trying to spell what he reads: 'A by itself spells a'; *t.h.e* spells the, and so on

'Snails: An oath, 'By God's nails!'

ostry:	inn
an:	if
horns:	sign of a cuckold
in good sadness:	to be serious
sack:	Spanish wine
muscadine:	another wine, muscatel
malmsey:	a strong, sweet wine
whippincrust:	hippocras, wine flavoured with spices

Act III Scene 1

We are informed by the Chorus of Faustus's journeys into space in search of 'the secrets of astronomy'. Marlowe's account of space once again draws upon the Ptolemaic system, with the earth at the centre, seven planets outside it, each orbiting the earth in its own special 'sphere'; outside these were the 'fixed stars', and outside these the *primum mobile*, the sphere which gave motion to each of the other spheres which it enclosed. All of this comprised the Universe. Above this was the 'empyrean', or heaven itself. Faustus goes from the moon, the first 'planet' outside the earth, all the way to the 'circumference' of the *primum mobile*, that is, to the very edge of God's abode. After this odyssey, he sets off from home on 'new exploits' of a more mundane kind, journeys across Europe and ends up in Rome.

NOTES AND GLOSSARY:

Primum Mobile:	*(Latin)* 'First Mover': the sphere beyond the other eight in the Ptolemaic system, which gives motion to all
subtle:	rarefied
prove:	put to the test
take some part of:	share in
this day:	the feast of St Peter and St Paul, 29 June

Act III Scene 2

(By Marlowe's collaborator, with later revisions.) Faustus informs Mephostophilis—but really the audience, of course—where they have travelled. Here we see language supplying the action which modern film audiences crave: the Elizabethans found mere language satisfying, because their imaginations were lively and hungry for detail.

Faustus asks if he is now 'within the walls of Rome'. Some scenery is called for here, perhaps the symbolic piece entitled 'the city of Rome' listed in Henslowe's diary among the scenery for the Rose Theatre (where *Doctor Faustus* was staged). Mephostophilis describes Rome.

Mephostophilis tells Faustus that 'This is the goodly palace of the Pope' and they are now supposed to be in 'his privy chamber'. There would be a throne here, needed for the Pope who enters in procession with his cardinals, bishops and so on and the anti-Pope Bruno *'led in chains'*. This would be a spectacular scene, splendidly costumed. Faustus determines to display his 'cunning' to the Pope, who is in turn displaying his power by using the anti-Pope as his footstool, while he sends his cardinals to consult about the appropriate punishment. Faustus and Mephostophilis follow them and put them to sleep, while the Pope addresses Bruno and condemns the Emperor who elected him anti-Pope. In overweening terms, which make him fair game for the mockery which follows, the Pope insists that he will depose the Emperor, adding: 'Is not all power on earth bestowed on us?'

Faustus and Mephostophilis re-enter, dressed as cardinals, give the council's verdict on Bruno and the Emperor, both condemned as heretics like the forerunners of the Protestant Reformation—a reference which would undoubtedly make the Pope appear villainous to the Elizabethan audience. Bruno is handed over to Faustus and Mephostophilis for punishment.

NOTES AND GLOSSARY:

Naples, rich Campania: Marlowe, following his source, wrongly identifies Campania in Italy with Naples

Maro: Publius Vergilius Maro (70–19BC), Latin poet, author of the *Aeneid*. He was buried at Naples

The way he cut: in the Middle Ages Virgil acquired the reputation of a sorcerer

sumptuous temple: St Mark's Cathedral in Venice

ordinance: armoury

pyramides: obelisk brought to Rome by the Roman emperor Caligula (AD12–41)

Styx ... Acheron ... Phlegethon: the three rivers of Hades, in classical mythology

situation: lay-out, whole extent of the city

triumphs: spectacular parades

antics: grotesques, clowns

crosiers: crosses carried by bishops

pillars: portable pillars carried as symbols of the cardinals' dignity

Saxon Bruno: a fictitious anti-Pope

state: throne

flourish: fanfare of trumpets

as the gods creep on with feet of wool ...: a proverb, 'God comes with leaden (woollen) feet but strikes with iron hands'

consistory:	meeting-place of the papal senate
statutes decretal:	papal decrees
council held at Trent:	the Vatican Council which was held between 1545 and 1563
synod:	general council
This proud confronter of the Emperor:	the Pope has captured the Holy Roman Emperor's nominee for the Papacy (Bruno)
excommunicate:	cut off from membership of the Roman Catholic Church
interdict:	forbidden
Pope Alexander ... Frederick:	Pope Alexander III (1159–81) compelled the Emperor Frederick Barbarossa (1152–90) to stoop to him
progenitor:	predecessor
basilisk:	a fabulous reptile, reputed to kill by its look
Pope Julius ... Sigismund:	fictitious characters
lollards:	heretics, like the followers of John Wyclif (c.1328–84)

Act III Scene 3

(Attributed to Birde and Rowley.) Mephostophilis tells Faustus to prepare himself 'for mirth', for Bruno has gone away on a winged horse and the 'sleepy' cardinals are ready to judge his case. Faustus asks to be made invisible, and he dons a special costume for this (Henslowe notes a 'robe for to go invisible in' in his diary).

The Pope, accompanied by King Raymond of Hungary, enters the council chamber and when it becomes clear that Bruno has escaped the puzzled cardinals are seized as traitors. A feast then begins, in celebration of the Pope's victory over Bruno, which Faustus interrupts by snatching the Pope's meat and wine; finally he *'hits him a box of the ear'* and the Pope leaves, convinced that a 'troublesome ghost' is to blame. Friars enter to sing the dirge of damnation over this 'ghost'. Faustus and Mephostophilis beat them and fling fireworks among them, and this farcical scene ends here.

The next eighteen lines (lines 108–25), spoken by the Chorus, were written by Marlowe's collaborator. They do not appear in the B-text, and were probably cut out by Birde and Rowley (in 1602). J. B. Steane thinks that these lines should really appear as a prologue to Act 4.* They tell of Faustus's return home to his questioning friends. His fame has spread 'in every land', even to the court of the Emperor Charles V, whither Faustus is now transported.

*See his edition, *Christopher Marlowe: The Complete Plays*, Penguin Books, Harmondsworth, 1969, p. 593, n. 45.

NOTES AND GLOSSARY:

Sennet:	trumpet flourish
censure:	judge
Furies' forkèd hair:	the Furies were the avenging spirits in Greek tragedy. The 'forkèd' hair refers to the tongues of the snakes on their heads
Pluto's blue fire:	the sulphurous flames of hell, Pluto being the god of the underworld in classical mythology
Hecate's tree:	the gallows
reserved:	kept safe
Hale:	drag
lade:	load
gyves:	chains
Fall to:	start eating
adry:	thirsty
lubbers:	clumsy fellows
dirge:	requiem Mass
Maledicat dominus:	*(Latin)* 'may God curse him'
stayed his course:	interrupted his journey
gratulate:	rejoice at
Carolus the Fifth:	the Emperor Charles V (1500–58)

Act III Scene 4

(By Marlowe's collaborator.) A comic scene, with Robin the Clown, Rafe [Dick], and the Vintner. (Compare 2.2.) It tells of the Vintner's demanding a silver goblet stolen from the tavern, while Robin conjures with Faustus's book. Mephostophilis, angry at being summoned by Robin, turns Rafe into a dog and Robin into an ape. The Penguin edition uses the longer A-text scene here, which has more comic 'business'.

NOTES AND GLOSSARY:

chafing:	friction, quarelling
wind her:	influence her (a pun on her name, Spit)
Ecce signum:	*(Latin)* 'Behold the sign', or 'Behold the proof'
gull:	fool him
Sanctobolorum ...:	this means nothing—it is a kind of Latinised nonsense-language
squibs:	fireworks
O nomine Domine:	bad Latin for 'in the name of God'
Peccatum peccatorum:	*(Latin)* 'Sin of sinners'
Misericordia pro nobis:	*(Latin)* 'Have mercy on us'

Act IV Scene 1

(An addition by Birde and Rowley, 1602.) The scene takes place at the court of the Emperor Charles V (who was Emperor from 1519 to 1536, that is, during the life of the historical John Faustus). This is simply an introductory scene. Two retainers, Martino and Frederick, discuss the arrival at court of Bruno and Faustus, who intends to show Charles (by magic) not only his ancestors but also Alexander the Great and his wife, Roxana. They call their friend, Benvolio, to tell him this news. He appears at the balcony *('above at a window, in his nightcap')*, expresses complete indifference to the magic, and remains where he is.

NOTES AND GLOSSARY:

voided straight:	emptied immediately
state:	throne
consort:	accompany
paramour:	lover; here, Roxana
took his rouse:	had a drinking bout ('carouse')
stoups:	measures
ope:	open (obsolete past participle)

Act IV Scene 2

(By Marlowe's collaborator, revised by Birde and Rowley.) Enter the Emperor Charles, with the anti-Pope Bruno, the Duke of Saxony, Faustus, Mephostophilis, and the two retainers from the preceding scene, Martino and Frederick.

The Emperor showers praise on Faustus, as 'Wonder of men, renowned magician', for freeing Bruno from their common 'enemy', the Pope. Faustus, promised even greater fame if Bruno comes to be Pope, dedicates himself to the service of Charles. Benvolio provides sarcastic comments, scoffing at Faustus, and declares that if Alexander and Roxana do appear he will 'be Acteon and turn myself into a stag', which is rather stronger than the modern expression, 'I'll eat my hat,' but is meant in the same incredulous way.

Faustus then makes Alexander and Darius enter, and there follows a piece of spectacular mime: they fight; Alexander wins, takes the Persian crown and is met by Roxana, whom he embraces and presents with the crown; then they advance and salute Charles, who leaves his chair of state to embrace them, but is warned by Faustus that 'These are but shadows, not substantial'. Charles verifies that Roxana has a mole on her neck, and expresses himself more pleased 'Than if I gained another monarchy'. Charles's wonder would be an effective way of securing the audience's also.

Faustus dismisses the show and draws attention to the horns he has placed on the head of Benvolio, asleep above. Charles wakens him, and they make fun of his predicament. Faustus agrees to remove the horns, but Benvolio must 'speak well of scholars'. While Faustus exists to share the emperor's political power, Benvolio vows revenge.

The student will find it useful to comment on the staging problem raised by this scene.

NOTES AND GLOSSARY:

professed:	openly declared
redeemed:	set free
chance:	fortune
ebon:	black (as ebony)
coster-monger:	one who sells fruit, fish or other goods from a barrow in the street
governor:	tutor
Acteon:	a mythological hunter who came upon the goddess Diana bathing and was punished for seeing her naked by being turned into a stag and torn to pieces by his own dogs
stays:	stops
compassed:	embraced
yon:	yonder, over there
footmanship:	skill in running
injurious:	insulting
o' this order:	in this manner
smooth faces and small ruffs:	In contrast to courtiers, scholars were often beardless and wore little collars

Act IV Scene 3

(An addition by Birde and Rowley, 1602.) Benvolio persuades Martino and Frederick to join in his revenge against Faustus. They plan to ambush and kill him, and they divide their forces for this purpose. Faustus enters *'with a false head'* and Benvolio falls on him, attacks him and cuts off his head. The three assassins gloat over the severed head, and plan to humiliate it publicly. Just as they turn to the Body, Faustus rises, and rather comically Frederick says: 'Give him his head, for God's sake!' (line 70). Faustus reminds him that for the duration of twenty-four years he is immune from death—clearly the first audiences were meant to be believed that he had, in fact, been decapitated: the trick was not meant to be obvious.

He then calls on Mephostophilis and other devils to torture the assassins, and they are taken away. Some of the other soldiers (who had divided from the main group) in the ambush then enter and Faustus spectacularly drives them off with 'soldierly' devils, with Mephostophilis wielding fireworks.

NOTES AND GLOSSARY:

let slip:	overlook
groom:	rascal
gambols:	frolics, jests
hie thee:	hurry
close:	hidden
bide:	wait for
in place:	on the spot
quit:	requite, repay
yoked:	held fast
policy:	trick
limited:	allowed
dally:	trifle with, delay over
caitiff:	wretch

He needs must go that the devil drives: a proverb
incontinent: immediately
Faustus strikes the door: that is, the door at the back of the stage. The setting is intended to be a wood, for this scene, but the Elizabethans were not consistent about such matters

Act IV Scene 4

(This is an addition by Birde and Rowley, 1602.) Benvolio, Martino and Frederick enter separately, *'their heads and faces bloody and besmeared with mud and dirt, all having horns on their heads'*. They meet and exchange exclamations of misery and awed recognition. They decide to shun society, out of shame, and retire to Benvolio's castle to live in obscurity.

NOTES AND GLOSSARY:

sped:	done for
spite of spite:	despite everything
sith:	since

Act IV Scene 5

(By Marlowe's collaborator, revised by Birde and Rowley.) The Penguin edition gives the A-text here, that is, the original, by the collaborator. This is longer than the B-version by about forty lines. It begins with a seven-line exchange in verse between Faustus and Mephostophilis, in which the passage of time is alluded to and Faustus says he wishes to return to Wittenberg. The rest of the scene is mainly in prose and concerns the Horse-courser (or horse-dealer) who comes to buy a horse from Faustus. Faustus warns the Horse-courser not to ride the horse over water, but after a brief interval, during which Faustus meditates on his damnation, and falls asleep in a chair, the Horse-courser re-enters, *'all wet, crying'*. Because he thought the horse must have had 'some rare quality' which Faustus did not want him to discover, he had ridden straight into a deep pond where the horse vanished and he was left astride a bundle of hay. He comes now to get his money back. He comes in muttering against Faustus, saying 'Doctor Lopus was never such a doctor (see below. Here we have direct evidence of a collaborator, since Marlowe died in May 1593.). He then tells of how the horse vanished, and demands to speak with Faustus, although Mephostophilis points out that he is asleep. Undaunted, the Horse-courser shouts in Faustus's ear and then pulls at his leg to wake him: the leg comes away in his hands (by a stage trick) and Faustus roars for the police. The terrified Horse-courser promises forty dollars more if he is allowed to go, and he runs away.

Wagner enters to announce that the Duke of Vanholt has invited him to his palace. Faustus accepts.

NOTES AND GLOSSARY:

Horse-courser:	horse-dealer. As such, he has an established reputation for dishonesty
you are well met:	I am happy to meet you
Ride him not into the water:	Running water breaks witches' spells
at any hand:	on any account
fatal time:	time allotted by Fate
Confound:	disperse
in conceit:	in mind
Doctor Lopus:	Dr Roderigo Lopez, physician to Queen Elizabeth I of England, was executed in 1594 for allegedly taking part in a murder plot against her
snipper-snapper:	servant
glass windows:	possibly 'spectacles'
bottle:	bundle
Hollows:	shouts

Act IV Scene 6

(An addition by Birde and Rowley, 1602.) This is another comic scene, set in a tavern. Robin (the Clown), Dick, the Horse-courser and a Carter order beer from the Hostess, and then proceed to tell stories of their experiences with Faustus, for example, the Horse-courser tells of the incident in the preceding scene. The Carter tells how he met Faustus as he was carting a load of hay, and agreed to take three-farthings for all the hay Faustus could eat; to his amazement, Faustus ate up the whole load of hay. After the Clown tells of his being given the face of an ape, all three plan to seek out Faustus, presumably to have revenge.

The farcical incidents that make up the action of IV.5, the narrative of IV.6, and the action of the next scene, IV.7, all have their basis in the narrative which is the source for the play in general, *The Historie of the Damnable Life, and Deserved Death of Doctor John Faustus* (1592). Silly as the incidents may appear, they are part of the original story.

NOTES AND GLOSSARY:

carter:	one who hauls goods for hire, using a horse and cart
on the score:	in debt
three-farthings:	three-quarters of an old penny
cursen:	Christian
quoth:	said
brave:	excellent

Act IV Scene 7

(By Marlowe's collaborator, revised by Birde and Rowley.) The scene is the court of the Duke and Duchess of Vanholt (at Anhalt, in Central Germany). It is written in prose. The Duke thanks Faustus for 'these pleasant sights', which apparently, included an enchanted castle in the air; and, responding to this appreciation, Faustus asks the Duchess, who is pregnant, to name something she most desires to have. The Duchess says she would like a dish of ripe grapes, but it is now January, the 'dead time of the winter'. Faustus sents Mephostophilis off on this errand, and he returns with the grapes instantly, to the great wonder of the Duke. Faustus explains about the southern hemisphere, where it is summer when it is winter in Europe.

The scene is interrupted by the noisy arrival of the comic characters from the preceding scene. They knock on the gate *'within'* the tiring-house and call out for Faustus, who asks the Duke to admit them as a source of 'merriment'. The Clown, Carter and Horse-courser then enter and behave as if they are still in a tavern, calling for beer. The Carter teases Faustus about his 'wooden leg', assuming that after the incident with the Horse-courser (in IV.5) he has only one sound leg. All are horrified when Faustus displays two sound legs. As they begin to abuse Faustus for what he did to them, he strikes each of them dumb, and they go out. This leaves the Hostess, who had appeared by magic to serve beer to the comic characters, demanding payment. Faustus strikes her dumb also, and she exits. The Duke and Duchess express their indebtedness to Faustus, for 'His artful sport drives all sad thoughts away'.

NOTES AND GLOSSARY:

for things are: for things that are (relative pronoun omitted)

meat: food

the year is divided into two circles ...: Marlowe here confuses the two hemispheres and the east/west distinction in geography

Saba: Sheba

bounce: knock loudly

coil: noise, disturbance

a fig for him: an insolent expression of contempt

varlets: rascals

wit: intelligence

commit: take to prison; but Dick understands the word in a sexual sense

gage: engage, stake

stand much upon: set great store by

courtesy: curtsy, bending the leg

colossus: the statue whose legs supposedly spanned Rhodes harbour

cozened: tricked

hey-pass and re-pass: juggler's exclamations

beholding to: indebted to

Act V Scene 1

This scene marks Marlowe's own resumption of the writing, though the collaborator may have helped or revised the scene. It also marks the return to a serious mood, indicated by the stage direction at the opening: *'Thunder and lightning'*. Mephostophilis leads devils with covered dishes into Faustus's study; he is, apparently, holding a banquet. His servant Wagner tells the audience that he believes Faustus's time must be nearly up, since he has made his will and left him all his wealth. He marvels, however, that Faustus should spend his time feasting among the students, if it is true that his death is near.

Faustus enters from the feast, accompanied by Mephostophilis and three scholars. Arising from their discussion as to who was the most beautiful woman ever, Helen of Troy is considered incomparable and the First Scholar asks Faustus to let them see her. Faustus agrees. Music sounds, Mephostophilis leads in Helen who walks over the stage and out again. Since the role was originally played by a boy (there being no actresses on the professional stage in England until after 1660), Helen's costume must have been sumptuous.

After expressions of appreciation, the three scholars leave; an Old Man, not seen before, then enters and appeals to Faustus to abandon magic and save his soul. To introduce a new character so late in a play is considered a fault, especially since we have no idea who he is, beyond his being close enough to Faustus to call him 'gentle son' and to speak with concern his 'kind rebuke'. (He appears in the source, *The Historie*, as a friendly neighbour.) Faustus is moved to despair at his words, and Mephostophilis hands him a dagger with which to kill himself. The Old Man interposes and says he sees an angel hovering over Faustus's head waiting to pour grace (spiritual assistance) if Faustus asks for it. Touched, Faustus asks the Old Man to leave him while he thinks upon his sins, and the Old Man goes, 'but with grief of heart,/Fearing the ruin of thy hopeless soul' (lines 66–7). Thus the Old Man serves to return the play to the theme of damnation.

Faustus upbraids himself, and expresses a sense of paralysis of will, 'I do repent, and yet I do despair' (line 69), rather like the state of Claudius, the villainous king in Shakespeare's *Hamlet*, who in a revealing scene at prayer finds that he wants not only the material things for which he committed murder but also salvation (see *Hamlet*, III.3.36–69). But when Faustus asks the basic moral question, 'What shall I do to shun the snares of death?' (line 71), Mephostophilis angrily calls him 'traitor' and threatens to tear him into pieces if he does not 'Revolt'. Immediately, Faustus yields, and offers to sign again with his blood his agreement with Lucifer. Mephostophilis urges him on, but it is not clear that Faustus actually goes through the business of signing with blood again.

Instead, he asks Mephostophilis to torment the Old Man for his advice which the 'greatest torment that our hell affords'. Faustus says 'our' hell here: he identifies himself with the place which earlier he had mocked at in disbelief (compare: 'I think hell's a fable,' I.5.130). Since he is now aware of hell he is also aware of the meaning of damnation, unlike the hubristic, sceptical Faustus of Act I. This awareness makes his failure to repent all the more moving and tragic.

In a complete change of mood, Faustus then asks Mephostophilis to let him have as his 'paramour' that same Helen of Troy lately seen. He gives as motive his desire to distract himself from the 'thoughts' that tempted him away from Lucifer. Here we see the direct opposite of Christian prayer, used to keep temptation at bay. The context in which Helen of Troy reappears, then, and the fact that she (a succuba, or demon) becomes Faustus's physical lover, indicates most clearly how Faustus blasphemes and chooses damnation.

It is hard, however, to bear this context in mind when considering Faustus's magnificent speech in praise of Helen, which follows, as she re-enters and passes over the stage between two 'Cupids' (actors dressed in classical fashion to represent sons of Venus, goddess of love). This speech, beginning with the awed question, 'Was this the face that launched a thousand ships....?', is deservedly regarded as among the finest poetry Marlowe ever wrote. Faustus marvels that such beauty should have caused such tragedy as the fall of Troy ('Ilium'), just as in modern poetry the Irish poet W. B. Yeats (1865–1939) marvels at the inspirational power of the woman he loved, his *femme fatale*, Maud Gonne, in a poem such as 'No Second Troy' and a play such as *Cathleen Ni Houlihan* (1902).

Faustus begs Helen to make him immortal with a kiss, meaning that any man who gains a kiss from such a woman must be raised to her mythic status; but there is also the secondary meaning, more ominous, that Helen is here a demon and can make Faustus a demon also. Some critics stress the secondary meaning, as if Marlowe meant to emphasise Faustus's sin of intercourse with a demon; but it may well be that Marlowe is being romantic, and uses the word 'immortal' as hyperbole, just as he did in *Dido, Queen of Carthage* when Dido said of Aeneas, 'For in his looks I see eternity,/And he'll make me immortal with a kiss' (*Dido*, IV.4.122–3).

After the word 'kiss' in *Doctor Faustus*, however, we are to imagine a pause followed by an actual kiss. Then Faustus declares that she takes his breath away, and he puts this with the typical hyperbole of the times: 'Her lips suck forth my soul: see where it flies' (line 100); and he asks for his 'soul' back, that is, he asks for another kiss, and declares that 'heaven is in those lips'—he wants to stay 'Here'. These are powerfully erotic lines; they describe a profane love, and establish a permanent value in a physical relationship. Undoubtedly, there is a hint of blasphemy in the use of such words as 'soul' and 'heaven', and in the idea of replacing their spiritual with a physical value—after all, the final line of the paragraph makes a value judgement: 'And all is dross that is not Helena'. Helen alone is pure, is refined gold, Faustus declares.

The Old Man re-enters, and apparently stands silently aloof until Faustus and Helen leave. Faustus continues his declaration of love to Helen, saying he will be her modern-day Paris, and will fight the old battles over again for her sake. Continuing in romantic vein he describes her as 'fairer than the evening's air,/Clad in the beauty of a thousand stars' (lines 110–11)—simple, but ardent language. He also finds her 'brighter' than lightning and more 'lovely' than the sun ('the monarch of the sky') when it is reflected in the blue waters of the spring Arethusa. After this magnificent speech of praise and reckless commitment, Faustus exits with Helen.

The Old Man then speaks. Modern editors include this speech, which is in the A-text but not in the B-text, because the action of Faustus requires some kind of comment, in view of his earlier remorse. The Old Man now comments rather like the Chorus at the end of the play; he makes clear that Faustus has deliberately *excluded* 'the grace of heaven' (line 118). In contrast, the Old Man himself withstands the 'ambitious fiends', confident that his faith will enable him to triumph. The contrast makes plain Faustus's failure.

NOTES AND GLOSSARY:

Determined with ourselves: decided

Sir Paris:	Paris of Troy is here given a medieval title, which associates him with romance, of the kind that is found in *The Knight's Tale* by Geoffrey Chaucer (*c.*1340–1400)
Dardania:	Troy
bereave:	deprive
amiable:	worthy of love
custom:	habit; that is, 'if sin does not become natural to you'
checking:	reproving, rebuking
do thee right:	pay you your due
vial:	phial, container for liquids
revolt:	turn back
drift:	drifting away from allegiance
clear:	entirely
topless:	immeasurably high
Helena:	the extra syllable is used to make up the metre of the blank verse line
sacked:	pillaged
Menelaus:	Helen's Greek husband, brother of Agamemnon. He was not 'weak' as such, and would have defeated Paris in combat were it not for the intervention of the goddess Aphrodite (in Homer's *Iliad*). Marlowe romanticises Paris's role
plumed crest:	feathered helmet
Achilles:	the great Greek warrior, who killed Hector and thus ensured the fall of Troy. In turn, he was killed by Paris, instructed by the gods to attack his one vulnerable point, his heel
Semele:	in Greek legend Semele asked Jupiter to appear to her in his full glory as a god; when he did so, she was consumed by the lightning which accompanied him
Arethusa:	in classical mythology, a nymph who was changed into a fountain
sift:	test

Act V Scene 2

To the sound of thunder, Lucifer, Belzebub and Mephostophilis emerge from hell to watch over Faustus's last night. They are thus silently on stage for the rest of this scene, unobserved by Faustus and friends (compare I.3). Mephostophilis sets the scene, so to speak, for Faustus's final agony by describing him as 'desperate' (line 12) and vainly trying to 'overreach the devil'. He also tells us that Faustus and Wagner have been concluding Faustus's last will and testament, and are coming in.

Wagner expresses his appreciation of Faustus's generosity, and they are joined by the three scholars. Faustus seems to them unwell, but he tells them he has 'damned both body and soul' (line 39), and cannot be pardoned. There follows a prose passage, rare in Marlowe's works, wherein Faustus takes a moving farewell of the three scholars, in the course of which he regrets ever having entered the academic world: 'oh would I had never seen Wittenberg, never read book' (lines 48–9). He confesses to his friends his present predicament, and urges them to leave him, in case they too might be endangered. They agree to go into the next room and pray for him. There is great pathos in this scene, largely achieved by the prose rhythms, with effective use of repetition, for example '... and must remain in hell for ever. Hell, oh hell for ever. Sweet friends, what shall become of Faustus, being in hell for ever?' (lines 53–5).

Mephostophilis, returning the scene to blank verse, twists the knife, as it were, in Faustus's wounded spirit by reminding him that there is 'no hope of heaven' (line 95), and when Faustus accuses him of robbing him of 'eternal happiness' Mephostophilis agrees that he was effectual in repeatedly turning him away from heaven. Bidding him despair, Mephostophilis exits.

The Good Angel and the Evil Angel enter, by separate doors, and they merely confirm, in contrasting tones, that Faustus is now certain to be damned. To the sound of music, a throne descends from the upper storey of the tiring-house. The Good Angel points out that Faustus might have occupied that throne in heaven, 'like those bright shining saints' (line 122; meaning that the throne was possibly decked with illuminated figures). But now that Faustus has 'lost', his Good Angel must leave him; and he exits, saying: 'The jaws of hell are open to receive thee' (line 125), which is the cue for the hell-mouth to be *'discovered'*. The throne would ascend before hell would be revealed. The Evil Angel urges Faustus to stare into 'that vast perpetual torture-house', which he then describes in detail, obviously pointing to specific features represented: 'There are the furies .... There are live quarters broiling on the coals .... This ever-burning chair/Is for o'er-tortured souls to rest .... These, that are fed with sops of flaming fire,/Were gluttons...' (lines 128–34). The impression of hell-fire is communicated powerfully through the language, reinforced by the visual aid of the 'Hell mouth' listed in Henslowe's inventory of scenery for the Rose Theatre (in his diary). The Evil Angel exits, as he says, until later ('anon') when Faustus will fall absolutely.

As the clock strikes eleven, Faustus is entirely alone, and he speaks his last, great soliloquy. Here, where Faustus's last hour is condensed into a few minutes of stage time, we are given as urgent and intense an expression of anguish as is to be found in all English dramatic literature. Here Marlowe's talent for the fine phrase and the powerful rhythm soars into greatness, as language and situation fuse to provide not formal eloquence, not mere rhetoric, but passionate speech.

The A-text version of Faustus's last speech is the one usually used in modern editions, as it is slightly fuller. The fifty-seven lines of the speech may be divided into four stages of development. First (lines 143–54), Faustus begins slowly, the partial line 'Ah Faustus' (only three syllables), indicating a pause of seven beats while he ponders on the fate expressed in the following two lines. These lines are made up of monosyllables which stress the stark facts of his situation, building up to the polysyllabic word which closes the sentence and emphasises the duration of his future punishment: 'perpetually'. There is a strong contrast here between finite time and infinite time. Faustus then appeals to the spheres to stand still, so that natural time might be arrested, and he appeals to the sun to rise again and keep midnight at bay. The imperative mood and the subjunctive mood ('let this hour be but/A year ...') express the wish, the need, to transcend the actuality of the present; but these tenses contrast with the future tense which is used almost immediately: 'the clock will strike./The devil will come,' and this sharp contrast between wish and realisation continues throughout the speech, as a means of intensifying and communicating the sense of tragic awareness Faustus possesses. There is a contrast also between the context of the Latin line he quotes from the poet Ovid (43BC–AD17) '*O lente, lente, currite noctis equi*', which refers to a lover's reluctance to see the dawn and leave his loved one, and Faustus's situation which is of complete solitude and lovelessness. The device of contrast thus effectively sharpens our sense of Faustus's time-bound and desolate predicament.

Second, at line 155 there is an abrupt change from third person to first person, as the feeling becomes more powerful, and grows more intense. One recalls here Faustus's first soliloquy, at the opening of the play, and his move from objectivity to subjectivity as he claimed a personal, independent identity. Now his subjectivity proves a burden: 'I'll leap up to my God: who pulls me down?' He has sold his 'self' to Lucifer, and so, far from winning freedom, he has enslaved himself to another objective presence whose force he foolishly had minimised. The vision he has now of Christ's blood in the sky ('the firmament' is both a more musical and a more cosmological word) only tears his heart by reminding him of what he has rejected. He calls on Lucifer (line 159) and the blood disappears ('Tis gone'). Immediately, he sees instead an image of the God of wrath (and of justice rather than of mercy), and asks to be hidden. The mountains will not fall on him nor will the earth open and swallow him, so he calls upon the stars to draw him up to the clouds so that when they controlled the weather Faustus's body might fall (as rain?) and his soul go upwards 'to heaven' (line 173).

Here, at line 173, the clock strikes the half-hour, and this marks the third phase of development in the speech (to line 192). As at the start of the speech, a short line (six syllables) indicates room left for a pause; the next line also has only six syllables, which doubles the effect. Then Faustus begs for his sentence to be commuted, but realises that 'no end is limited to damned souls.' The eternity of the sufferings is here stressed. Faustus then wishes that the Greek philosopher Pythagoras' (c.582–c.507BC) theory of metempsychosis were true, for then his soul would find lodging in some animal, and would be 'dissolved' after the animal's death. This is a stage further in his desire for escape—into gradual annihilation. He curses his parents for begetting him, then curses himself, then curses Lucifer for depriving him of 'the joys of heaven' (line 192). This last phrase should be compared with Faustus's use of it when he scoffed at Mephostophilis about hell: 'What, is great Mephostophilis so passionate/For being deprived of the joys of heaven?' (I.3.83–4). Then Faustus scoffed; now he is in deadly earnest, too late.

The fourth and final phase comes with the clock striking twelve. Faustus's language becomes frenzied: 'Oh, it strikes, it strikes!' (line 193). He calls on his body to 'turn to air' and his soul to be changed 'into little water drops' and fall into the ocean, never to be found. This is the final stage of his expressed wishes: total annihilation. To the sound of thunder, the devils then enter, and gabbling repetitively to God and the devils he asks for time. He promises to burn his books (the sources of his temptation) and in the same line he is confronted with his old servant-spirit and he says, quite simply, 'Ah, Mephostophilis!' (line 200). How pregnant that last line is! Mephostophilis has been waiting twenty-four years for this glorious moment. It is the moment of truth. Faustus is taken off into hell.

The student may find it useful to compare the Faustus who appears in the first scene of the play with the Faustus who speaks the last soliloquy. It is also rewarding to consider the use made of *time* in Marlowe's expression of Faustus's tragic situation, with particular reference to Faustus's last speech.

NOTES AND GLOSSARY:

Dis:	a name sometimes given to Pluto, god of the underworld in classical mythology, and hence also to the lower world itself. Marlowe freely mixes pagan (classical) references and Christian references.
demean:	conduct
fond:	foolish
Gramercies:	thanks
imports:	signifies
abjured:	forsworn, rejected
stays:	stops
vain:	empty
bill:	deed
Music while the throne descends:	the music room was above the balcony in the scene building or 'tiring house' of the Elizabethan public stage. Above the music room was the machine room from which 'properties' such as a throne could be let down by pulleys, as if from the heavens. Ben Jonson (1572–1637), the playwright, poked fun at this sort of spectacular theatre in the Prologue to his *Every Man in His Humour* (1616)
affected:	followed
Hell is discovered:	some representation of hell was revealed by the drawing of a curtain before the central opening in the 'tiring house'. 'Discovered' is a technical term as used in Elizabethan stage directions
O lente, lente ... equi:	*(Latin)* 'O slowly, slowly run, O Horses of the night'. The words are Ovid's (*Amores* I, xiii, 40), of a lover wishing to prolong the night in his mistress's arms
One drop...soul:	a reference to the Christian doctrine of redemption. By shedding his blood on the cross, Jesus Christ saved mankind from hell, and continues to save if man repents of his sins
You stars...my nativity:	Faustus ascribes a fatal influence to the stars, a common Elizabethan belief
labouring cloud:	swelling, increasing (as if pregnant)
watch:	clock
limited:	fixed definitively
metempsychosis:	the doctrine of the transmigration of souls, as traditionally ascribed to the Greek philosopher Pythagoras

still:	always
quick:	alive
books:	here, of magic

Act V Scene 3

(As this scene is not in the A-text, it may not be by Marlowe, but there is some doubt on the matter.)

Three scholars enter next morning to visit Faustus. The First Scholar comments on the stormy night just passed, and on the 'fearful shrieks and cries' hears, and he prays that Faustus has 'escaped the danger'. But the Second Scholar sees Faustus's mutilated body, and the Third Scholar remarks: 'The devils whom Faustus served have torn him thus' (line 8)—one must imagine some false limbs strewn here and there where the hell-mouth was. The Third Scholar describes how he heard Faustus call for help around twelve o'clock, and how the 'house seemed all on fire' at the time. The Second Scholar calls on his friends to give Faustus's 'mangled limbs due burial' (line 17), even though his death was such as to make Christians lament. Because Faustus was a scholar 'once admired' he will have a proper funeral, attended by 'all the students'. There is pathos in this scene, with its quiet but sombre mood coming after the stormy, high-pitched anguish of the preceding scene.

NOTES AND GLOSSARY:

methought:	it seemed to me
for he:	because he
wait upon:	accompany on its way
heavy:	sorrowful

Epilogue

The Chorus who first introduced Faustus to the audience, and who served twice more to describe his progress, now reappears to make a final judgement and offer a warning. Such a practice was common in morality plays, but was not usual in Elizabethan tragedy. Another example is seen, however, in the anonymous domestic tragedy *Arden of Faversham* (c.1591), where one of the characters, Franklin, provides the epilogue.

The Chorus announces, in metaphorical language, that Faustus has been cut off, his potential for scholarship destroyed. 'Faustus is gone' (line 23): the phrase, occupying only a half-line, falls with the abruptness of a judicial statement. The other half of the line orders the audience to 'regard his hellish fall', which (the following lines say), deriving from diabolical agency, should be an example to wise people not to practise 'unlawful things'. The Chorus thus sums up the tragedy, and offers a moral reading of Faustus's 'fall'.

NOTES AND GLOSSARY:

Apollo: the Greek god of poetry and song; here he is associated with learning or genius

Laurel bough: The laurel or bay tree was always associated with Apollo

sometime: once (not 'sometimes')

exhort: urge

forward wits: daring intellects

only to wonder: be content with merely wondering

Terminat hora diem, Terminat Author opus: *(Latin)* 'The hour ends the day, the author ends his work.' That is, all things come to an end. The motto was probably added by the first printer

Part 3

Commentary

Tragedy

The first thing to be clear about in studying *Doctor Faustus* is that it is a tragedy. The Greek philosopher Aristotle (384–322BC) has provided in his treatise on poetry and drama a valuable definition of tragedy which may assist us in clarifying our thoughts about Marlowe's achievement:

> Tragedy, then, is an imitation of an action that is serious, complete, and of a certain magnitude; in language embellished with each kind of artistic ornament, the several kinds being found in separate parts of the play; in the form of action, not of narrative; through pity and fear effecting the proper purgation ['catharsis'] of these emotions.*

Aristotle, of course, was writing about classical Greek tragedy, in the fourth century before Christ, but his concept was nevertheless the one employed, with modifications, during the whole period of the Renaissance. Through the Italian commentators, Aristotle's theory of poetry spread to England, where it became the basis of formal aesthetics—seen, for example, in Sir Philip Sidney's (1554–86) *The Defence of Poesie* (1583). Therefore, it is by no means irrelevant to call upon Aristotle, and the classical idea of tragedy, while discussing and interpreting Elizabethan tragedy. But the reader must, at the same time, take into account also the particular conventions and traditions of which the English dramatists made use.

Two points must be emphasised. First, a tragedy is the *imitation of an action*, which reminds us that a play is primarily concerned not with characterisation but with some situation within which the human will tries to master human destiny: it is the motive or impulse of the hero which provides the action, and it is the action which is symbolic of the human predicament. Therefore, the place to begin in any exploration of tragedy is to ask the question, 'what is the action here?' by which is meant not 'what is the plot?' in the sense of the story in general but 'what is the central motive or objective of the hero?' In the present case, the action of *Doctor Faustus* may be said to be: 'to be absolute' or 'to have infinite pleasure.' The will of Doctor Faustus is directed towards

*S. H. Butcher, *Aristotle's Theory of Poetry and Fine Art with a Critical Text and Translation of the Poetics,* Dover Publications, New York; Constable, London, 4th Ed., 1951, p. 23.

possessing infinite knowledge, infinite power and infinite pleasure. He discovers that this is impossible, given the finite nature of man's existence, the fact that time controls man's experiences. Doctor Faustus had made a contract which allowed him absolute mastery in his chosen fields of science and pleasure, and by its very nature that contract had a time clause. Therefore the hero's *motive* or impulse dragged him inevitably into failure. This course or track, from success to failure, from the heights to the depths, is the tragic action.

Secondly, the nature of 'catharsis' must be clarified. The translator uses the word 'purgation', and he might even have said 'laxative', since Aristotle used 'catharsis' as a medical term. The function of tragedy as Aristotle saw it was deliberately to foster passions in the audience so that these might be siphoned off and the spectators be left in a state of emotional equilibrium, of euphoria. This explains why audiences can derive pleasure from the presentation of suffering and even of disaster on stage (or in a film): there is a process of identification with the hero (the protagonist), whose sufferings excite both sympathy and terror, and this experience leaves the spectator drained but also relieved, and even feeling elevated. Some commentators would say that catharsis is a purifying experience, that the spectator feels not only relief and pleasure, but also intellectual and spiritual heightening. It is, at any rate, commonly accepted that tragedy is not a depressing experience but in fact a pleasurable one. We should always examine the ending of a tragedy carefully to see whether and to what extent catharsis is achieved. If the ending strikes us as unrelievedly depressing or pessimistic or, on the other hand, as incredibly optimistic and implausible, then either we have misread the play or it is seriously flawed as a tragedy. Catharsis, the final emotional impact of a tragedy, is one of the greatest experiences of all art, and is therefore a vital criterion in the assessment of a play. In the discussion of *Doctor Faustus* below, we shall attempt to establish that, in spite of the fact that the hero is damned at the end, the play provides us with the sense of release and illumination which characterises catharsis.

The medieval background

Marlowe straddles two traditions: the medieval and the modern. His play can be seen as an expression of man emerging from a set of old beliefs and giving expression to new and radically different values, as yet untested and without a convenient social structure. It is a play about man in transition, torn apart by the twin forces of his rejection and his aspiration. To understand this middle ground (where the play takes place), the reader must understand Marlowe's medieval heritage.

The drama of the Middle Ages, in England as on the Continent, was didactic and highly moral in outlook. Tragedy as such was unknown, but poets such as Geoffrey Chaucer (*c.*1340–1400) put forward an idea of tragedy which clearly implies an example *(Latin, exemplum)*. In the prologue to 'The Monk's Tale' Chaucer defines tragedy as a story of a man 'that stood in great prosperity' but has fallen 'out of high degree/Into misery, and ends wretchedly'. This medieval notion, known as the *De Casibus* (concerning the misfortunes of tragic heroes) type, insists that tragedy is a warning, a fall with a message. The examples were usually drawn from history, as can be seen in *The Mirror for Magistrates* (1559), a collection of 'tragic' cases, drawn from English history, intended to show the fickleness of Fortune. The first English tragedy in blank verse, *Gorboduc* (1561), was a 'mirror' play of this kind; being a play about a civil war resulting from unwise division of a kingdom by the father of two sons, it was a warning to Queen Elizabeth that the succession to the throne of England was crucial, if order were to be maintained.

There was, then, an orthodox view of tragedy and its function, which Marlowe could hardly avoid knowing or drawing upon. From that point of view, *Doctor Faustus* contains within it a 'mirror' for all scholars; it provides an example of the fall which can occur unless Faustus's ways are avoided. Linked up with this emphasis, and rather at odds with it, is the stress in *Doctor Faustus* on the romantic discoverer, the daring adventurer, who is admirable in both courage and sensitivity to the values of the imagination. This Renaissance side of the play, this celebration of the questing, flesh-loving man, sounds a new note—that of yearning to be free of the shackles of the medieval frame of mind, and in the conflict between the two worlds or the two philosophies (medieval and Renaissance), the tragedy takes place.

Another feature of medieval drama upon which Marlowe drew, and against which he also provided an underlying note of protest, is the morality play. This kind of drama, which flourished in the fifteenth century but survived well into the sixteenth, depicted in allegorical terms man's struggle for salvation. For example, man might be shown tempted by World, Flesh and Devil: these abstract concepts would be represented on stage by actors. One of the best-known morality plays is *Everyman*, which describes the last hours of a man who, God informs him, must die that day; God sends Death as a person with this message. Everyman argues with Death and says he is not ready to go; he offers a thousand pounds if Death will come back another day. But Death is adamant: it must be today. Yet he will allow a friend to accompany Everyman, if the latter can find one. His friend, Fellowship, enters, asks what is wrong and claims he would do anything for Everyman, but on hearing about the journey he excuses himself and runs off. Next come Kindred and Cousin, Everyman's close relations, who also protest loyalty but subsequently run away. So Everyman turns to Goods, the figure representing his material possessions, and argues with him—in vain. Goods tells him his role is to destroy, not to save; he laughs and runs off. The only one willing to help Everyman is Good Deeds, but he is too weak (from Everyman's neglect) and lies on the ground; he sends Everyman to his sister, Knowledge, instead, and she makes the famous commitment:

> Everyman, I will go with thee, and be thy guide,
> In thy most need to go by thy side.

She takes Everyman to see Confession, and after a time he returns to Good Deeds, who is then able to rise and go with Everyman to the grave. A character called the Doctor enters and in his speech makes plain the moral of the whole play.

Doctor Faustus, like Everyman, is under sentence of death. He is visited by the Good and Evil Angels, each urging him in a contrary direction. He meets Lucifer, Belzebub, and the Seven Deadly Sins, representative characters who lead Faustus into the path of damnation. And in the end, after his death, the Chorus speaks in a style entirely similar to that of the Doctor at the end of *Everyman*—it is a warning speech ('regard his hellish fall'). In several ways (the use of the Chorus/Narrator, use of allegorical characters, use of hell as the place where Faustus must end) Marlowe's play has links with the traditional morality play. But there are also unorthodox features: Faustus is an individualist, not an Everyman; his will is fixed on pleasure and racked by doubts at the same time (this self-division is new); there is a Calvinistic determinism in the play which is foreign to the morality play (in the latter salvation was always a likely outcome, as the play was a trial and a conversion sequence); admiration is elicited for the sinner. In short, the outline of the morality play lies behind *Doctor Faustus*, but it bursts through the pattern to establish a new, heroic form, which challenges orthodoxy rather than reinforces it.

The staging of *Doctor Faustus*

The third matter to understand in studying *Doctor Faustus* is the kind of stage for which Marlowe wrote. The first public, professional theatre was opened in London only in 1576, perhaps a decade before Marlowe began to write. Theatres sprang up quickly once they were allowed by law, and theatre-going became the craze of the Elizabethan period. It was an extraordinarily eclectic kind of theatre, part medieval and part modern. It was in the round, that is, it used a bare stage thrusting out half way into the auditorium, and the stage was surrounded on three sides by the audience; the fourth side was made up by the 'tiring house' or scene building, which usually had three entrances on to the stage: one at either side and a larger opening in the centre. Hence this kind of stage direction: *'Enter at several doors* BENVOLIO, FREDERICK *and* MARTINO' (IV.4). Sometimes a curtained area was used for an individual scene, for instance, perhaps for Faustus's study in I.1; such scenes were 'discovered', that is, revealed by the drawing of a curtain. Compare the stage direction, *'Hell is discovered'* (V.2.125), implying that a piece of scenery is suddenly revealed. There is no reason to suppose, as some have argued, that there was an inner stage, set behind the centre opening of the scene building, revealed by the drawing of a curtain. Such an arrangement would hide details from at least part of the audience. It is more likely that a booth or pavilion was placed in front of the central opening for 'discovery' scenes. In general, little scenery was used (the language, the poetry, did most of the work of the modern scenic artist); what was used was medieval in style, taking the form of 'mansions' or symbolic structures which could be arranged on stage at will (or transported to Court or to the provinces when the players travelled). An upper level, a balcony in the scene building, could be used in conjunction with the stage platform. Use of this upper level is particularly effective at the end of *Doctor Faustus*: although no stage direction specifically says so, it seems likely that Lucifer and Mephostophilis go up to the balcony and stay there, looking down on Faustus during his last agony. Three levels, hell, earth and heaven, are suggested by the sub-stage, the stage and the upper stage areas, and so the idea of a complete or cosmic picture of life is suggested by the simplest possible means. Evidence of the medieval heritage of the Elizabethan stage is supplied by Philip Henslowe's diary. Henslowe owned the Rose Theatre, on the Bankside in London, and it was here that *Doctor Faustus* was staged in the 1590s; Henslowe lists his scenery and costumes for the year 1598, and these include 'a dragon for Faustus', a 'city of Rome', and a 'Hell mouth'. The costumes were quite elaborate (and costly), and we must imagine quite an effect of pageantry in the spectacular scenes, such as the Pope's procession in III.2.

The general staging principle was what is termed 'successive' staging, the different parts of the stage standing for different locations, according to the changes of scene demanded by the action of the play. This arrangement is, of course, unclassical (violating the so-called unities of time and place) and a contemporary critic, Sir Philip Sidney, for this reason poked fun at the Elizabethan staging methods. Having criticised the academic tragedy *Gorboduc* for its deficiencies, he continued:

> But if it be so in *Gorboduc*, how much more in all the rest, where you shall have Asia of the one side and Afric of the other, and so many other under-kingdoms, that the player, when he comes in, must ever begin with telling where he is, or else the tale will not be conceived? Now ye shall have three ladies walk to gather flowers, and then we

must believe the stage to be a garden. By and by we hear news of a shipwreck in the same place, and then we are to blame if we accept it not for a rock. Upon the back of that comes out a hideous monster, with fire and smoke, and then the miserable beholders are bound to take it for a cave. While in the meantime two armies fly in, represented with four swords and bucklers [shields], and then what hard heart will not receive it [the stage] for a pitched field?*

Sidney would have preferred the more classical, 'monoscenic' stage, without changes. But the Elizabethan method allowed for rapid movement and flexible handling of the narrative. *Doctor Faustus* can span time and space with ease, thanks to the simple conventions of the popular stage. We have to accept, however, that Marlowe could and did make huge demands on audiences willing to 'piece out our imperfections with [their] thoughts', to use Shakespeare's appeal in the Prologue to *Henry V*. It was an age of wonder, when people's imaginations easily took fire, and responded to the poet's least suggestion. Today, the excellent techniques of film and television have rather spoiled our responsiveness to the word, or to bare suggestion. For the Elizabethans, *Doctor Faustus* must have seemed wondrous, solely from its suggestions of outer space, paranormal experience and instant travel to exotic places. It is necessary for us to keep alive some such kind of awe, child-like or not, if we are to respond adequately to the romantic and sensational qualities of Marlowe's imaginative excursion. The last thing that should be in our minds is realism; since Marlowe's play depends for its effect on the imaginative collaboration of its readers or its audience. After all, the play was staged in broad daylight, out of doors, with little chance of achieving atmosphere in modern ways. There is evidence that performances of *Doctor Faustus* in Elizabethan times achieved frightening authenticity; real devils were reported on stage, and it is said that the actor Edward Alleyn (1566–1626), who played Faustus, retired early from the stage as a result of an unsettling experience when playing the role. Imaginative participation in the play has its own rewards, no doubt.

To sum up, Marlowe's theatre was part medieval, in its retention of symbolic scenery and its neglect of the classical unities. This sort of theatre may also be called 'modern' inasmuch as it was profane rather than sacred. It was dedicated to entertainment, not to improvement of the audience's morals. *Doctor Faustus*, in such a setting, is seen as primarily art, not doctrine.

---

* Sir Philip Sidney, *The Defense of Poesie*, in *Literary Criticism: Plato to Dryden*, ed. Allan H. Gilbert, Wayne State University Press, Detroit, 1962, pp. 449–50.

The characters

The hero

To a considerable extent, *Doctor Faustus* is a one-man play. The characterisation, that is to say, is not at all as rich or varied as that which Shakespeare's drama was later to reveal; Marlowe seems mainly to have interested himself in a single type, the towering, Dionysiac figure, and to neglect or leave to collaborators the depiction of minor characters.

Doctor Faustus himself, then, even more than Hamlet in the play bearing his name, dominates the whole play. He is a scholar, but one who soon finds excessive the constraints of formal academic studies. In the opening scene, he takes up and rejects as unsatisfying philosophy, medicine, law and theology. It is his rejection of theology ('divinity') that stamps him as arrogant and proud. The Chorus, just before the opening scene, compares him to Icarus, son of Daedalus, who, in Greek legend, put on artificial wings, made with wax, and flew too near the sun: the image is one of daring and of hubris (a Greek word in origin meaning excessive energy or pride). Faustus, like Icarus, dares to break with orthodox doctrine and to launch out on his own towards the unknown, seeking mastery over human knowledge. By studying black magic, or necromancy, he aspires to absolute power: 'All things that move between the quiet poles/Shall be at my command' (I.1.55–6). His pride is combined with soaring ambition far in excess of what is proper to man as finite being. Blasphemously, Faustus claims that 'A sound magician is a demi-god' and he aspires to possess divine powers himself. Thus this opening scene reveals already the tragic potential of this scholar, whose pride draws him into a rash attempt to transcend his finite being. Thereafter, his fall, like that of Adam—the archetype of all Christian tragedy, as the poet John Milton (1608–74) shows in his epic *Paradise Lost* (1667)—illustrates the folly of the attempt.

Faustus is also a man of courage. The common man usually shrinks from the sort of action which the tragic hero casually undertakes. One sees this clearly in Greek drama, where the Chorus (made up of common men, representative of the audience) magnifies the courage of the hero by its own timidity. Faustus is his own Chorus, inasmuch as he is well aware of the enormity of what he is doing in making a study of black magic. Thus, defiance rings out loudly in his line, 'This night I'll conjure, though I die therefore' (I.1.165). His courage is seen in his steadfast determination to conjure, in spite of the thunder which sounds on the night of his first attempt (I.3), and in spite of his being informed by Mephostophilis that 'the shortest cut for conjuring/Is stoutly to abjure all godliness/And pray devoutly to the prince of hell': Faustus replies that he has already done so (I.3.55) and insists that:

> This word 'damnation' terrifies not me,
> For I confound hell in elysium.

That is, he holds the view that hell is merely the happy abode of the dead, the 'elysium' of classical literature. The courage shown here, which is not the bravado of the ignorant but the recklessness of the over-educated, is a characteristic that Faustus displays to the very end. However we may question Faustus's pride and stubbornness, there is no denying that in the final scenes of the play he displays a manliness which is truly admirable. In this regard he displays the Renaissance quality of *virtú*, or noble forbearance even in desperate circumstances. Compare the lines in Shakespeare's *Macbeth*, descriptive of the death of the traitor, the Thane of Cawdor:

> Nothing in his life
> Became him like the leaving it. He died
> As one that had been studied in his death
> To throw away the dearest thing he owed
> As 'twere a careless trifle.   (I.4.7–11)

Faustus is a Renaissance man in two other respects also: in his appetite for knowledge and in his love of beauty.

As soon as he has signed away his soul, Faustus settles in to a dispute with Mephostophilis. He asks numerous questions, pressing all the time for clear and unequivocal answers. Here he shows himself the intellectual, the man from the university relentless in his drive after knowledge. Mephostophilis' answers about hell do not satisfy him, and he is invited to visit it to see for himself—which he later does (III.3.70). Next he disputes about astrology, and is impatient with Mephostophilis for supplying only well-known details about the heavens—'freshmen's suppositions' he calls such data (II.1.55). He wishes to know far more, and accompanies Mephostophilis on a strange odyssey—a wondrous journey—through space, in search of pure knowledge (as described by the Chorus, III.1). He then goes on a guided tour of Europe, ending at Rome. To an Elizabethan audience, such a journey would appear breathtaking, but quite in accordance with the new spirit of adventure which had led to the discovery of the Americas. Faustus is a traveller of many kinds, and his restless odysseys mark him off as an explorer who recognises no boundaries to human endeavour. Wittenberg is his university: the place where Martin Luther started the Reformation. To Elizabethan audiences, such reference would suggest a brave rebel.

Faustus's love of beauty is bound up with his love of pleasure, his love of power and his love of classical literature. Hedonism, or the philosophy of pleasure, governs and undermines his motives. In this area Faustus at first shows himself to belong to the Middle Ages, and later (this is part of his development) to belong to the Renaissance. At first Faustus welcomes necromancy as a study which promises 'a world of profit and delight.' This is almost the orthodox definition of the function of literature, by classical standards. Faustus is at first orthodox enough to want only 'profit' or illumination; his reaction to the first 'show' which Mephostophilis puts on for his entertainment is to ask, 'what means this show?' He is given the art-for-art's-sake reply: 'Nothing, Faustus, but to delight thy mind' (I.5.83). He learns, then, to look on art and literature Satanically, as self-sufficient pleasures. In Act II he is shown the pageant of the Seven Deadly Sins, and remarks, 'Oh, this feeds my soul', and is reminded, 'in hell is all manner of delight' (II.1.177–8). In a sense, this is a joke, an irreverent claim—much as George Bernard Shaw (1856–1950), the Irish playwright, was later to make in the hell scene of his *Man and Superman* (1905)—that hell is where the fun is. Faustus must be seen as the sort of pleasure-seeker who is also a rebel against the more repressive or ascetic tenets of Christian belief, whereby pleasure is sinful. In his exercise of power, also, Faustus displays a rebellious attitude. To a degree, he uses his magical powers frivolously, for entertainment rather than for social change; it will be recalled that part of Faustus's ambition is to be 'great emperor of the world' (I.3.104), but we see him only playing tricks with the power he possesses. There is, however, a progress in his use of his powers. In the first exercise of them, at the Pope's palace, there is nothing but mockery in his attitude—he enjoys fooling the Pope and his cardinals in a gleeful, schoolboyish manner. In the second episode, at the Emperor's palace, Faustus is received seriously, except for the mocking of Benvolio, who is suitably punished: here again Faustus is Puckish in his exercise of magical powers. But in the third episode, there is no mockery at all (apart from the intruders, who are literally silenced); the Duke and Duchess of Vanholt simply express their appreciaion of Faustus's skill repeatedly, and the Duke concludes, 'His artful sport drives all sad thoughs away' (IV.7.133). Faustus's progress is upward in this regard, and the pleasure he derives is balanced by the pleasure he gives as entertainer. Here, indirectly, Marlowe proposes also a defence of the poet or playwright, seen as Renaissance and not as medieval artist—an illusionist who 'drives all sad thoughs away'.

Faustus's love of classical literature makes even clearer his position as Marlowe's representative, a poet surrogate. Classical literature was regarded as profane in medieval times but, of course, in the age of the Renaissance Greek and Latin texts found ready and enthusiastic readers. Faustus says:

Have not I made blind Homer sing to me
Of Alexander's love and Oenon's death?

And hath not he that built the walls of Thebes
With ravishing sound of his melodious harp
Made music with my Mephostophilis?   (II.1.26–30)

Here the tone is that of the complete enthusiast, the profane romantic. References to Paris of Troy ('Alexander'), the nymph who loved him (Oenon) and Amphion, whose music charmed the stones that built Thebes, are summed up in the one word 'ravishing'. The pleasure Faustus takes would be of a kind frowned on by Christian teaching for its kinetic sexual content. (You might compare Stephen Daedalus on Aquinas's theory in James Joyce's (1882–1941) novel *A Portrait of the Artist as a Young Man*, (1916).) More indicative of Faustus's indulgence is the passage where he asks to see Helen of Troy, 'To glut the longing of my heart's desire' (V.1.89). His admiration for Helen is not disinterested, as was advocated by the many academies or centres of learning which encouraged a cult of love and beauty during the Renaissance. His response is indeed overwhelmingly poetic, in the well-known lines appreciative of Helen's beauty:

Was this the face that launched a thousand ships,
And burnt the topless towers of Ilium?
... Oh, thou art fairer than the evening's air,
Clad in the beauty of a thousand stars.
                                    (V.1.97–8, 110–11)

This remarkable passage, one of the most beautiful in English literature, is no less than a hymn of praise to womanly beauty. Faustus, however, is not content to admire Helen; he wishes to make love to her also. By magic, Helen's form is rendered palpable, and exits with Faustus to be his 'paramour' (V.1.116). It is clear that here Faustus is guilty of 'demoniality', since Helen is a succuba. The abuse of poetry is seen here in this shocking conclusion, as the abuse of power was seen in Faustus's frivolous playing with disbelievers.

Faustus, in summary, is a rebel who sells out to the 'pleasure principle'. He indulges fully his sensual and intellectual appetites, and tries to suppress or ignore a third force in life, the terrible power of the irrational, the unknown. This opposing power is shared indiscriminately between hell and heaven—there is no basic difference in how obedience and conformity are demanded. Thus it is Mephostophilis who says, towards the end: 'His store of pleasures must be sauced with pain' (V.2.17), while the Angel points out that Faustus has lost 'celestial happiness/Pleasures unspeakable' (V.2.117). Absolute hedonism is not permissible to mortals either by heaven or hell—as the Evil Angel says, 'He that loves pleasure must for pleasure fall' (V.2.140). In this way, Marlowe suggests that there is 'no exit' for the human being, with his infinite longings for beauty, knowledge and love, short of a partial denial of his own nature.

Finally, Faustus is a character divided against himself. If he were absolutely committed to pleasure he would be uninteresting, a mere playboy and not a tragic figure. Because he has an inner life, where there is constant conflict between despair and rebellion, he has tragic potential. It is invariably consciousness of evil, a sharp moral perception, that provides a hero with tragic status. And Faustus is fully, intelligently aware that black magic is evil, and that his contract with Lucifer will damn him. He struggles against this awareness, oscillating between confidence and capitulation to despair in such a way that he stands revealed, like Hamlet in the later play, as a man agonisingly torn between scepticism and idealism. Faustus is a sympathetic character, that is, a hero who absorbs our interest and moral understanding, because he reflects a dilemma which is universal, the eternal quarrel within man between the desires of the spirit and the desires of the flesh. Almost every scene in the play illustrates this inner conflict, which is Marlowe's great contribution to English tragedy. And in the end, Faustus puts his essential dilemma as clearly as can be:

> Hell strives with grace for conquest in my breast.
> What shall I do to shun the snares of death?
>
> (V.1.70–1)

'What shall I do?' is the moral question which continues to echo across the centuries. Faustus, in that sense, is the new Everyman.

Other characters

Although the other characters in *Doctor Faustus* are not very sharply individualised—in contrast to Shakespeare's usual method of making even the smallest part stand out—a certain amount of variety among the types and levels employed can be described. It must be borne in mind that the authorship of these lesser characters may derive from a hand other than Marlowe's. Yet it is clearly part of the design of the play that there should be different levels of characterisation, from high to low and from serious to absurd. This range serves to give to the play a sense of social extension, as if Faustus were at the centre of quite a busy world. Thus there are university characters, court characters and religious characters, suggesting a broad spectrum of society. Within each of these we can observe a symmetry—there are good groups and bad groups. Thus there are two good, or concerned scholars, offset by Valdes and Cornelius, two bad scholars (who seduce Faustus into necromancy). Similarly at both the Papal Court and the Imperial Court there are figures of authority and figures who carry out the orders. A similar dichotomy exists between Lucifer and Mephostophilis, and in a broad sense between the serious characters and the comic (the Clown, the Horse-courser). The Good Angel and the Evil Angel also contrast symmetrically, and the Old Man contrasts with Faustus himself, the young man.

This pattern of characterisation, with its hierarchical structure and its contrast of high and low, serves to keep clear before our minds the fact that the central conflict involves dilemma, two rivalling ways of thought and experience. As it is a play about the essential duality of man, his leaning towards the intellectual and spiritual life and his simultaneous leaning towards the physical and sensual life, it is appropriate that the characterisation should reflect the basic opposition.

Marlowe takes care not to give Faustus's colleagues, whether good or bad, a prominent place in the action. They appear in very few scenes; Valdes and Cornelius appear only in one (I.1) and though Valdes might be expected to reappear to teach Faustus how to conjure in I.3, he does not. The two good scholars who contrast with these appear in I.2, when they go off to the Rector hoping that he can 'reclaim' Faustus, and are not heard from again until V.1, where they add one more to their number, so that for most of the play they are off stage. They do play a significant role in Act V, surrounding Faustus with a circle of concerned friends unable to help him: this brings out the pathos of his position, isolated as he is by the choice he made. It humanises Faustus, who otherwise might be regarded as a cold intellectual, that he has such warm friends as the three scholars who offer to stay with him to the end; but 'lest you perish with me' (V.2.78) he persuades them instead to keep vigil in the room adjoining the scene of his final agony. Such discipleship indicates the heroic appeal of Faustus.

Leaving aside the clowns and low-life characters, who may not be Marlowe's creations, it is worth observing that the other human characters can further be divided into those who admire Faustus and those who scoff at him. This distinction holds whether the characters are in high or low position. The effect is to make Faustus the central attraction, the star, the one who (as in a fantasy) must and can prove that he is the 'greatest'. This is the technique which Marlowe had already displayed in his earlier play, *Tamburlaine*, where an obscure shepherd rises by innate abilities to become emperor of the world, overcoming all sceptical and effete opposition on the way. It is a technique of reflection: all other characters have the function of reflecting upon the emergent power and significance of the hero.

The supernatural characters deserve special mention, however. The Good and Evil Angels are merely functional. They appear in I.5, II.1, and V.2, always together and always very briefly; they are like signs pointing to contrary messages, 'too late', and 'never too late'; they are

dramatic for their sudden and ghost-like appearances and dis-
appearances. Mephostophilis is much more fully drawn as a character.
While he is but a servant, and thus responsive to Faustus's commands,
he also has a personality of his own. He is in his own way an orthodox
fellow, a follower of Lucifer with unswerving loyalty; and it is ironic that
he should tell Faustus to pronounce the spells 'devoutly' for full effect
(I.5.165). He insists on a full legal contract with Faustus, which marks
him as officious; and he has no time for the idea of a wife for Faustus—
marriage, he says, is 'but a ceremonial toy' (I.5.153). He can be irritable,
as when he refuses to answer the question, 'who made the world?'
(II.1.69ff.), and is happiest when busy, as in the scenes at the Papal court
(III.2 and III.3) or driving off Faustus's opposition with fireworks
(IV.3). He is unhappy if forced to reflect on his actual state, as in the
famous lines where he describes hell as an internal experience:

Why, this is hell, nor am I out of it.
Think's thou that I that saw the face of God
And tasted the eternal joys of heaven,
Am not tormented with ten thousand hells
In being deprived of everlasting bliss?

(I.3.76–80)

Next in this beautiful passage, Mephostophilis confesses to 'terror' (line
82) at the consciousness of the everlasting loss he continues to suffer.
Such a passage serves to emphasise the nature of the self-destruction
Faustus is about to cause. But such moments of self-exposure are rare on
Mephostophilis' part; usually he is a civil servant and no more, an
underling whose job is his life, and so far he is contemptible. This side of
his character serves to highlight Faustus's superiority, since Faustus has
that *sprezzatura*, great carelessness and freedom from orthodox
observance of rules, which the hero in tragedy invariably manifests.
When Mephostophilis finds Faustus difficult, he sends for his boss,
Lucifer. There is something comic about this reliance on higher
authority. And in the end, Mephostophilis seems aware how vastly
superior Faustus is to himself; he displays the meanness and spite which
the small-minded usually exhibit towards those once-great who are
sliding towards ruin. 'Fond wordling,' he describes him, without a trace
of sympathy, 'now his heart blood dries with grief' (V.2.13), and he
rejoices at having robbed Faustus of eternal happiness (V.2.100).

Lucifer lacks the dignity and sense of greatness we might expect. (He
has none of that sublime power of Milton's Satan, for example.) He is a
businessman, intent on the full terms of the contract Faustus makes. He
comes running whenever the business seems to need him, and he
smooths over the problems. For example, he comes bustling in to
Faustus as the latter calls on Christ in Act II, and having rebuked him

continues: 'Talk not of Paradise or Creation, but mark this show. Talk of the devil and nothing else' (II.1.110–11). He is, in a sense, a parody of the deity, a slightly ridiculous figure. His final arrival, up through the stage, has this quality: 'Thus from infernal Dis do we ascend/To view the subjects of our monarchy' (V.2.1–2). It is virtually impossible to make an entrance from below stage with anything like imperial dignity. In contrast, the throne which descends from above, bearing hosts of the saints for Faustus to wonder at (V.2.116), shows forth the genuine majesty of God and the glory of heaven.

Themes and imagery

The three major themes in *Doctor Faustus* are the aspiration or longing of the hero for the infinite; the over-reaching or excess of the hero's drive; and the deadly contract between human and demon elements.

The imagery serves to highlight these themes, meaning by 'imagery' figures of speech, especially metaphors, that recur in such a way as to form a significant pattern. The image of flight highlights Faustus's soaring aspiration. The Chorus on his first appearance mentions Icarus, son of Daedalus, who dared to try the air on man-made wings, recklessly flew too near the sun and was destroyed. This image sums up the tragic fall of Faustus. Elsewhere in the play (in III.1 and III.2) we hear of his actual flights in space, in the company of Mephostophilis. These wondrous journeys, these odysseys, make clear his boundless thirst for knowledge. The image reappears at the end, in Faustus's final soliloquy: 'Oh, I'll leap up to my God: who pulls me down?' (V.2.155). Faustus now finds that he is earth-bound, indeed bound to go *beneath* the earth (for the spatial location of the stage hell is below), and the force that pulls him down is the same as the one that gave him flight: so we *see* how he has collaborated in his own destruction. The over-reaching theme is impressed by the food and feasting imagery. The Chorus on his first appearance says of Faustus: 'He surfeits upon cursed necromancy' (line 25), meaning he 'feeds excessively'. Faustus in reproach tells himself, 'The God thou servest is thine own appetite' (I.5.11); he responds to the pageant of the Seven Deadly Sins with the cry 'Oh, this feeds my soul' (II.1.177), and expresses a desire to partake of the Pope's feast, 'Whilst I am here on earth let me be cloyed/With all things that delight the heart of man' (III.2.59–60). Wagner reports that Faustus does 'banquet and carouse and swill/Amongst the students' recklessly (V.1.6–7), and before the end Faustus begs Mephostophilis 'To glut the longing of my heart's desire' by bringing him Helen (V.1.89). Mephostophilis says Faustus's pleasures must now be 'sauced' with pain (V.2.17) which again introduces the food image and Faustus confesses to his friends that he is suffering not from a 'surfeit' in the ordinary sense (indigestion), but 'A surfeit of deadly sin, that hath damned both body and soul' (V.2.39–40). Finally, when Faustus is shown hell's interior by the Evil Angel his attention is drawn to the 'gluttons' that 'loved only delicates,/And laughed to see the poor starve at their gates' (V.2.134–5), which perhaps reminds us of the Seven Deadly Sins again, where Gluttony featured and cursed Faustus: 'Then the devil choke thee' (II.1.162). This train of images underlines the qualities of excess and irresponsibility which apply to Faustus's pursuit of his ambition.

The deadly contract between human and demonic elements is made grimly emphatic through the imagery of blood. Early on Faustus dedicates himself to the power of evil by promising an altar and church to Belzebub and the offer of 'lukewarm blood of new-born babes' (I.5.13–14)—a truly horrific image. The contract he makes with Mephostophilis must be signed with his own blood. This intensely theatrical moment is rendered even more sensational when Faustus's arm fails to yield blood, and he sees this as a dreadful omen: 'My blood congeals and I can write no more!' (I.5.61). In panic he speculates, 'why streams it not that I may write afresh?' (I.5.65). It is as if humanity protested against the evil implicit in the fearsome contract. The blood streams again only when Mephostophilis brings coals from hell to warm the congealed blood—a symbolic gesture. As the play draws to a close, the image of blood expresses the human suffering of Faustus with great force. 'Now his heart blood dries with grief,' gloats Mephostophilis (V.2.13). Faustus himself, in his anguish, wishes he could weep blood rather than tears, as a measure of his human sorrow: 'Gush forth blood instead of tears' (V.2.59–60). And in his last, great speech, Faustus has such a vision of the divine mercy which he cannot reach that (like Macbeth in Shakespeare's later play) he thinks he sees a sign in the air:

See, see, where Christ's blood streams in the firmament.
One drop would save my soul, half a drop... (V.2.156–7)

The use of the verb 'streams' here echoes the passage where Faustus made the original contract and his blood congealed ('why streams it not?' I.5.65). In this manner, the imagery unifies the theme of a fatal decision made and makes its significance powerfully expressed. The last we hear of Faustus, from his friends, is that he has been torn limb from limb, like some sort of sacrificial victim, and they vow to give the 'mangled limbs due burial' (V.3.17). This dismemberment and blood-shed provides a Dionysian conclusion modifying a Christian tragedy.

Language

Marlowe was one of the outstanding poets of the Elizabethan age—'his raptures were all fire and air,' the poet Michael Drayton (1563–1631) said of him. He scoffed at the poor state of tragedy upon his first arrival as a dramatist in London—what he called 'jigging veins of rhyming mother-wits' (*Tamburlaine*, Part I, Prologue, line 1), or the jog-trot rhythms of the ballad metre. The following is an example from Thomas Preston's (1537–98) *Cambises* (1569) of what Marlowe reacted against—this is the death scene of the tragic villain Cambises:

> I feele myselfe a-dying now, of life bereft am I,
> And Death hath caught me with this dart, for want of blood, I
>   spy.
> Thus gasping heer on ground I lye, for nothing I doo care.
> A just reward for my misdeeds my death doth plain declare.
> (lines 1167–70)

This is crude, artificial and somewhat ludicrous. Marlowe replaced the rhyming ballad metre with iambic pentameter, the five-foot unrhymed line, and he used it to register the thoughts or emotions of his hero in a psychologically credible way. Blank verse, as iambic pentameter is also called, works best in longer passages (taken as paragraphs), and Marlowe was able to introduce considerable subtlety of diction and rhythm by extending a speech in this manner. The outstanding examples from *Doctor Faustus* are the lines on Helen (V.1.97–116) and Faustus's last soliloquy (V.2.143–200). In each of these passages the language is rendered intensely dramatic by its close association with the speaker's situation and feeling. In the former of the two, Faustus speaks in awe, his sense of Helen's beauty first finding apt expression in the question form, containing the daring metaphors 'launched' and 'burnt':

> Was this the face that launched a thousand ships,
> And burnt the topless towers of Ilium?

'Topless' adds vast scale to the reference: Helen's beauty was so great she caused such mighty towers to fall (in war); the alliteration ('t') unifies the second line, where the rhythm demands that the voice continue to 'Ilium' before the sense is complete. Marlowe's placing of individual words is masterly: he arranges the pause within a line (where normally it would occur in the middle) just where some word calls for special emphasis—for example, 'Her lips suck forth my soul: see where it flies', where the pause after soul, followed by the imperative 'see' calls attention, as with a gesture, to the speaker's specific experience. The line is then no longer fanciful, but a powerfully dramatic expression of the actual loss of Faustus's soul. Likewise the repetition of 'come' in the next line, 'Come, Helen, come, give me my soul again', embodies in its rhythm the intensity of the character speaking—it is not merely an ornamental device. In the speech as a whole, the notion of giving the soul, and of declaring that 'heaven is in those lips' (line 102), carry a special irony, given the actual basis of Faustus's contract with Mephostophilis. The song of praise is also a piece of daring blasphemy.

In the other speech, the final soliloquy, the urgency of Faustus's situation is reflected in both rhythm and diction. 'One bare hour' (line 144) provides three long stresses—signifying the stark fact that time is running out. In contrast to the simple, stark language in this line comes the word with which the next line ends—'perpetually',—its rhythm rippling on to emphasise the notion of eternal time. This skill, this control over language and rhythm is seen all through this speech, which deserves detailed study (see above, pp.38–9). The words chosen, and the order given them within the verse pattern (notice the words with which Marlowe ends a line, for instance, and the effect this positioning has) define clearly and vividly the situation of the man in anguish, longing for a reprieve to his 'sentence' and intelligently aware that this is impossible. Marlowe is not merely filling up lines to make up a metrical pattern, as happens in *Cambises*; he uses interjections ('Oh', 'Ah',), repetitions, questions, imperatives, exclamations, all sorts of rhetorical tricks to focus attention on the individual, Faustus's sense of imminent death and damnation.

Form and structure

The tragedy of Faustus is told within a strict time scheme. The form involves a contract made and its payment falling due; thus there is a period of 'suspense' during which Faustus has his will and pleasure, winding down to the scene where the action relates directly to the striking of the clock as his last day draws to its inevitable end. The form is thus closely bound up with the operation of time. Any play, of course, has its duration in time (the time of performance) but a very special intensity is gained when a writer makes this duration an aspect of the tragic action itself. In *Waiting for Godot* (1952), for example, by the Irish playwright Samuel Beckett (*b*.1906), the protagonist's activities seem pathetic in relation to the determinism (the crushing control) of relentless time. Faustus 'passes the time' agreeably enough—for himself as for us—but he is never entirely free of the nagging consciousness that 'time's winged chariot' is hovering near. He is also torn apart by his conscience, his awareness that he has made a mistake in turning away from God. This awareness provides an undercurrent to his whole progress, making the final stage of the action seem the necessary conclusion: we see a man caught in a vice, which he willingly and knowingly helped to set up and tighten.

The one-man play, the fate of the Herculean hero (to use the title of Eugene M. Waith's book*), is also part of the structure. The fact that

The Herculean Hero, Chatto and Windus, London, 1962.

Faustus has no family, no wife, and only his colleagues for friends, places him in peculiar isolation. The tragedy is a stark confrontation between himself and his God.

Doctor Faustus, then, comprises the following conventional features of the morality play: (i) use of a Narrator (Chorus); (ii) externalising of the Tempter/Resistance opposition (Good Angel, Evil Angel); (iii) the Old Man, the human monitor; (iv) use of the Hell mouth—strong visual emblem of orthodox Christian morality.

Marlowe, however, also uses the following features which rather go against the morality play tradition: (i) the resolution of Faustus, his determination to ally himself with the powers of evil; (ii) the determinism within the action, which appears Calvinistic: Faustus is not granted the grace of repentance; (iii) admiration is evoked for Faustus, in spite of his sinfulness.

A third feature of the form is the use of comedy. In general, Elizabethan dramatists did not scruple to mix comic and tragic elements in one play. True, Sir Philip Sidney condemned this usage in his *The Defense of Poesie* which was written in 1583 but not published until 1595 (when both he and Marlowe were dead). Having condemned contemporary ignorance of the 'three unities', Sidney goes on to say:

> But besides these gross absurdities, how all their plays be neither right tragedies nor right comedies, mingling kings and clowns, not because the matter so carrieth it, but thrust in the clown by head and shoulders to play a part in majestical matters, with neither decency nor discretion, so as neither the admiration with commiseration nor the right sportfulness is by their mongrel tragicomedy obtained.

The mixing of what he called 'hornpipes and funerals' Sidney found unforgivable. But this is a pedantic view. In the public theatres, audiences apparently greatly enjoyed this mixture of genres. The title-page of Preston's *Cambises* reflects this unabashed admiration for variety: *A Lamentable Tragedy Mixed Full of Pleasant Mirth, Conteyning the life of Cambises King of Percia*. The play itself combines a serious theme with a considerable amount of horseplay from comic characters, picturesquely called Ruf, Snuf and Huf. Marlowe did poke fun at the likes of *Cambises* for its naïvety but, whether or not he himself wrote the comic scenes in *Doctor Faustus*, he apparently gave sanction to their inclusion. In that regard he was simply recognising the public love for diversion, even while attending at a serious play. After all, in the Middle Ages audiences were granted interludes of farce and spectacle even in the course of the story of the Birth, Passion and Death of Jesus Christ, the most sacred of dramas. The mixture, therefore, had deep-rooted traditional associations.

It is possible to distinguish two kinds of comedy in *Doctor Faustus*.

First there are those scenes where some touch of comedy appears, and these seem undoubtedly to be Marlowe's own composition; and then there are scenes where farce or slapstick are uppermost, and these would appear to be either by his collaborator or by later interpolators. The first category includes I.3 and I.5. In each of these there is a mordant note, a touch of penetrating satire, alongside the serious episode in hand. When Faustus conjures first, a devil enters and is told to go away and come back as a Franciscan friar, since 'That holy shape becomes a devil best' (I.3.25), which is the kind of joke one might expect from a university 'wit' like Marlowe. In that same scene Mephostophilis confesses to 'terror' at some of Faustus's 'frivolous demands', and is urged to have 'manly fortitude' by Faustus, a mere human (line 85). The inversion here of the expected roles—Faustus is the one who should be afraid—has the sort of incongruity one associates with comedy. In a similar scene, after Faustus has signed the bond, he turns from unwelcome questions about hell to ask instead for a wife. Mephostophilis tries politely to dissuade him, but then agrees to fetch one 'in the devil's name' (I.5.149). Then a devil enters, dressed like a woman, wielding fireworks, and Faustus instantly changes his mind. The joke plainly associates a wife with a devilish firebrand, and is again akin to undergraduate satire. This impish humour reminds us, perhaps, that the great critic and poet T. S. Eliot (1888–1965) described Marlowe's *The Jew of Malta* as 'tragic farce'. The same sort of adolescent but vicious humour is visible in some scenes of *Doctor Faustus* as characterised *The Jew of Malta*.

In other scenes in the play, probably not written by Marlowe, comedy appears either as light relief from the serious theme or as a grotesque version of it. Wagner is mildly amusing in I.2 in using the special vocabulary of the schools when merely telling the scholars that Faustus is at dinner. But in the next scene we see him recruiting a new disciple (the Clown), in a manner which reflects upon and parodies Faustus's own relationship with Valdes and Cornelius. The frivolousness of the Clown's interest in black magic—he wants to be turned into a flea, so as to have access to 'the pretty wenches' plackets' (petticoats—I.4.59)— throws into relief the desperate urgency of Faustus's own motives. These low-life scenes, continued in II.2 and III.4, form a sub-plot to Faustus's main action. It is a sub-plot, however, which has only a slight content, and which exists mainly as an end in itself. The last-mentioned scene continues the vein of I.4, as Robin the ostler plans to use Faustus's conjuring book to gain himself the sight of 'all the maidens in our parish' dancing naked before him (III.4.4–5). He wins a fellow-ostler, Rafe, to sorcery by promising him the desirable Nan Spit for his 'use'. This commonplace bawdry may be compared with Faustus's desire for a wife (I.5.144) and with the passage about Helen (V.1.88ff.). The juxtaposition of low and high romance provides a special kind of irony. At other times this irony is entirely absent and the comedy is sheer slapstick. When Benvolio plans revenge on Faustus for placing horns on his head, Faustus amuses himself by entering with a *'false head'* (IV.3.37) and after Benvolio *'Cuts off his head'*, Faustus pretends to be dead and then rises to frighten and torment Benvolio and his supporters. Mephostophilis helps the sense of fun by throwing fireworks among Faustus's enemies here—as often in these scenes. Faustus's dealings with the Horse-courser (IV.5) have their basis in the *Faust-book (The Historie of the Damnable Life)* and make excellent farce; but the continuation of this incident, featuring the Horse-courser's meeting with the Clown, Dick and a Carter in a tavern (IV.6) and their subsequent attempt to embarrass Faustus at the Duke of Vanholt's palace (IV.7), carries the joke too far. Tiresome though some of this material is, Faustus disposes of all such nuisances as Benvolio and the Horse-courser with complete superiority, by the end of Act IV. No comedy is allowed to dilute the intensely serious atmosphere of Act V. Marlowe was too much the artist not to know when comedy (and even the grotesque) would be entirely out of place.

Interpretation of the play

There is less debate over the meaning of *Doctor Faustus* than there is over Shakespeare's *Hamlet*, but nevertheless it is well to be aware that there are in existence two equally valid and cogent interpretations of the play. According to one view, *Doctor Faustus* is a straightforward warning against the dangers of atheism, the tragedy residing in the needless self-destruction of a man full of sinful pride. In other words, this argument runs, Marlowe's play is an account of sin and retribution, in orthodox Christian terms. On the other hand there is the view that the play attacks orthodox Christian belief, and presents Faustus as the victim of a malevolently designed universe. In other words, this argument runs, Faustus is a hero who exposes the Satanic structure of life itself. Two opposing interpretations are here deliberately simplified, so as to invite the reader to think carefully about the character of Faustus, and the end to which he comes. Before attempting to decide to which of these opposing interpretations the reader might be persuaded to incline, it is essential to clarify two points.

First of all, we must be extremely cautious about using what we know about Marlowe's own character and beliefs when interpreting his play. Whereas art is based upon experience, it is also, as both T. S. Eliot and W. B. Yeats have testified in modern times, impersonal. That is, the artistic creation itself need have no exact correlation with the life of the artist. We cannot assume that if a man is an atheist he will write an atheistic play; or, conversely, that if a play seems entirely atheistic that its author was necessarily an atheist (an argument which surrounds Shakespeare's *King Lear*, for example). The tendency, therefore, to read into *Doctor Faustus* the known facts about Marlowe's mockery of sacred things, and his reported atheism, must be resisted. The play must stand on its own terms, and be interpreted, so far as is possible, from internal information.

A second point to be borne in mind is that literature, and especially tragic literature, is not in the business of providing answers, but, rather, in the business of formulating questions. To read a text in the right, or critically legitimate, manner the reader must clear out of his mind the notion of a 'lesson' to be abstracted or a message to be delivered. Art is, in the poet John Keats's (1795–1821) phrase 'a thing of beauty', a thing made, a 'well-wrought urn' as the poet John Donne (1572–1631) calls a poem. It exists for its own sake, but it has the effect of arousing feelings in the beholder or reader. The function of criticism is to examine the techniques by which the art object is 'thus and not otherwise', and to assess whether or not and in what degree the work arouses the feelings proper to good art. What these feelings are will depend on the nature or genre of the art object. The feelings appropriate to tragedy are obviously not going to be the same as those appropriate to comedy or to satire; and, accordingly, one estimates the effectiveness of a tragedy in relation to the feelings of pity and terror communicated by its effect as a whole.

The action of *Doctor Faustus* takes the form of a rising and a fall—a soaring climb to master the infinite, followed inevitably by a headlong, irreversible rush into ruin. The terms in which this action is presented are unequivocally Christian. There is no doubt whatsoever but that Faustus agrees, willingly and without provocation, to hand over his immortal soul to Lucifer, prince of hell, in exchange for supernatural powers to last for the duration of twenty-four years. Admittedly, Faustus disbelieves in hell, and calls it a mere 'fable' (I.5.130), but Mephostophilis testifies strongly to its reality, and it is this reality which Faustus is at length forced to recognise. As with Shakespeare's Macbeth, who knowingly enters into a life of evil and goes against his own better judgement, his own conscience, so also Faustus persists in his cause deliberately, in spite of what his conscience tells him. Both characters damn themselves. It is not a matter of a tragic error, as is usual in Greek tragedy (for example, Oedipus unknowingly killed his father and unwittingly married his mother); in Elizabethan drama free will is of the essence of the tragic fall.

Yet all tragedy seems to involve a process of self-recognition. The tragic hero usually comes to a perception of a moral order to which he had been blind, or which he had arrogantly ignored. So it is with Faustus. It can be said that his basic fault or sin is Pride, which at first takes the form of 'presumption', that is, he aspires to god-like knowledge and powers—the sin of Lucifer himself as described in the Bible. What makes Faustus attractive is his restless impatience with limitations, of human knowledge and of human capability; we are drawn to admire his daring. But it is also clear to us from his own 'aides' and soliloquies that this daring is foolhardy and dangerous. And so we anticipate a retribution, a Nemesis or pattern of reaction from whatever moral order governs the universe—in this case the Christian God. The pattern of retribution pleases us because it contains justice. It has within it the force of inevitability. And when the pattern is almost complete, Faustus himself sees the justice of it, and this is why he refuses to repent but falls instead into despair. Despair is the other side of presumption: both are sins of pride. Thus, it might be said that in time Faustus comes to see his own presumption and then he despairs. It is sometimes asked why there is no release for Faustus, why no mercy is shown him at the end.

Some commentators, following W. W. Greg's essay, 'The Damnation of Faustus' (1946), take the line that Faustus has turned himself into a spirit or demon by signing away his soul in Act I, and that there is thus no possibility of his ever reverting to completely human form. This would explain lines such as Lucifer's, 'Christ cannot save thy soul, for he is just' (II.1.88). But it would mitigate the tragic status of Faustus himself, which depends on his being free to act as he will. We cannot accept the argument that Faustus turns into a demon. His despair, rather, urges him to allow himself to be destroyed, almost in the manner of a suicide—for example, the suicide of Othello, who kills himself out of a spirit of justice, when he recognises his enormous error. This, perhaps, is what makes Faustus finally admirable, in spite of the evil way he has wilfully chosen: he has a keen sense of his impending 'execution', but he does not try to evade it. He does not involve anyone else in his destruction either; notice the firmness and consideration with which he puts his three friends out of the room before his last speech—he wishes to no harm to come to *them*. Marlowe preserves his hero from any significant injury or crime against his fellow-men all through the play—unlike Macbeth, or even Marlowe's own Tamburlaine, Faustus kills nobody. Therefore the final picture we have of him is not of a villain or a tyrant (as Macbeth and Tamburlaine both become), but of a pitiable scholar who has made a complete mess of his life and his talents. He is human to the last, his feelings not corrupted or hardened, and so he retains our sympathy.

Finally, the last great speech of Faustus reminds us that he is not a godless man at all, not an atheist, but a man whose pride sank him into damnation. Today we tend to regard an atheist as indifferent to the supernatural question. Faustus is never indifferent. His conscience is never at rest; he merely goes against its promptings. It is more useful to regard Faustus as a saint turned inside out than as an atheist in our modern sense of rationalist, scientist, a complete non-believer. For a comparison one would have to turn to the novels of Graham Greene (*b*.1904), such as *The Power and the Glory* (1940), in which the sinner accosts damnation in despair, but is characterised always by his *caring* about the question, which causes him great anguish. *Doctor Faustus* is, in the same way as are Graham Greene's early novels, a deeply religious work, and its hero is essentially a deeply spiritual man.

Thus it is probably best to regard *Doctor Faustus* as holding in tension the two conflicting attitudes, the orthodox Christian view as expressed by the Chorus, and the rebellious Renaissance view, the humanist anthropocentic emphasis. Marlowe's sympathies, as the final agony of Faustus clearly shows, are for the rebel, but he does not in any way evade or minimise (much less mock) the Christian idea of judgement for Faustus's rebellion. Marlowe arrives at what one critic* calls 'tragic balance', or a sense of the horror of his hero's destruction within a moral order which may be harsh and may allow a devilish rival order to thrive but which ultimately affirms justice. This tragic equilibrium communicates itself to the audience as a form of catharsis, the purgation of pity for the suffering Faustus and terror at his eternal ruin.

*Una Ellis Fermor, in an essay entitled 'The Equilibrium of Tragedy' (1945).

Part 4

Hints for study

The nature of the choice

The point mainly to be borne in mind in relation to this tragedy is that it is a spiritual one. Perhaps the scenes of conjuring and 'horse play' tend to divert our attention from this central fact. But diversions they are, frivolous or spectacular as the case may be. And in the end the play is fundamentally concerned with man's spiritual destiny, his individual relationship with his God.

It is helpful, therefore, to reread the play in order to dwell only on the serious scenes, where Faustus ponders and agonises over his condition. Art matters only in so far as it is serious, in so far as it urges us to take the gift or miracle of life seriously; because when we do we confront the great questions of human existence which have perplexed thinkers from the beginning of civilisation. If we find ourselves unable or disinclined to ponder such questions as 'what is the purpose of existence?', or 'is there a meaning in being?', or 'is there a life after death?', then we should probably first leave *Doctor Faustus* to one side until we have given such matters some thought. The play uses the idiom of serious discussion; if we have not learned the 'language', no amount of commentary will avail to explain the play to us. Because, basically, the play itself only serves to explain *ourselves* to us, as creatures with a spiritual destiny.

In the opening scene, the stages of Faustus's revolt are quickly gone through, but they should be slowed up and contemplated like stills from a motion picture. We may see then that Faustus is a restless, intellectual figure, at odds with the formal rigours of education, impatient with the plodding path open to man who wishes to climb the ladders to worldly success and to higher knowledge. Philosophy? Is this what he wants to spend his time on? No. It is too barren for his impatient spirit. The way to wisdom is not for him. (In the end, of course, like every tragic hero, Faustus discovers wisdom through suffering.) Then he rejects the study of medicine. It is too limited, in his view; it leaves man 'still but ... a man'. We begin to see now that Faustus, though easy to sympathise with, is looking on his career in an altogether selfish way. His egoism is something that should alert us to danger. A discipline such as medicine or, indeed, law (which Faustus considers next) calls, as we all acknowledge, for considerable qualities of dedication to others and the public good. Would Faustus have made a good doctor or a good lawyer?

A brilliant one, in either case, we may feel sure; but one hungry for reputation at all costs, and likely to use his profession rather than serve it. This opening scene, then, shows us the dangerous egoism, pointing to megalomania, underlying Faustus's romantic aspirations.

The fourth and final profession Faustus considers is theology ('divinity'), the study of the nature of God himself, or, in broader terms, Christian philosophy. We will find it harder to sympathise with Faustus here. All students in medieval and Elizabethan times were monks, in minor orders; the successful were intended for ordination. The medieval love affair between the French philosopher Peter Abelard (1079–1142) and his pupil Héloise takes its poignancy from his being a clergyman, and therefore not free to marry. Faustus, like Abelard, is clergyman as well as scholar—and already he has acquired a reputation as a scholastic figure (as we learn from the Chorus, lines 15–19, and from his friends' comments, in I.2.2). Therefore when he considers 'divinity' here he is examining the very roots of his being and his calling. In a few quick strokes he dismisses it—'Divinity, adieu!' (I.1.48). Because of two texts from the Bible which he brings together (John, 1:8 and Romans, VI:23), he concludes that Protestant man must sin and so must be damned. Martin Luther (1483–1546), the German leader of the Reformation, who was also a student at Wittenberg in the early sixteenth century, wrestled rather more painfully than this with his doubts since these went far beyond fears for his own skin and into basic questions of eternal truth. Faustus dismisses orthodox Christian doctrine simply because it seems to present an insoluble problem of logic: mortal man is sinful, and sin is damnable, therefore mortal man is to be damned. On this basis he opts out and chooses necromancy or black magic as the solution to his personal problem.

The close study of this opening scene, then, rewards us with insight into the representative nature of Faustus, the extent to which he embodies our own frustrations and restlessness. 'The mass of men lead lives of quiet desperation,' the American author David Henry Thoreau (1817–62) has written. Faustus shows us this kind of desperation. He is man in a crisis, having lost his sense of conviction and thus his sense of direction. The alternative he chooses, moreover, reminds us that there always is open to us a comparable choice, a door forbidden but passable; and if we choose it we are testing the very roots of our belief, and must expect upheaval and possible annihilation.

The Devil and the see-saw

The essence of the tragic choice made by Faustus lies in the contract made with Mephostophilis. Although he scoffs at the idea of hell, he willingly binds himself to Lucifer in lieu of special powers granted for twenty-four years. But even before he signs the contract with his own blood Faustus oscillates between feelings of despair and euphoria. Thereafter, he wavers so often that a reader might be forgiven for thinking that Faustus did not know his own mind. The see-saw of his doubt and recovery is part of the 'furniture' of the play.

In medieval drama the Devil was one of the most popular characters, a licensed prankster, whose antics were inevitably terminated by his exit into a spectacular hell-mouth, with one or more hapless victims with him. The din and the smoke which would then issue from hell would thrill the audience with child-like wonder, half in approval, half in awe. The Devil was a grotesque figure, an animated gargoyle, polarising the saints and virtuous men whose destinies lay in evasion of his 'low' behaviour and in pursuit of higher company. His costume was distinctive, with tail, cloven feet, animal mask and horns, and he carried a trident to herd the damned into hell.

Records show that *Doctor Faustus* employed devils quite in the medieval manner. As late as 1620 a commentator says, 'there indeede a man may behold shaggehayr'd Devils runne roaring over the stage with squibs in their mouthes, while Drummers make Thunder in the Tyring-house, and the twelve-penny Hirelings make artificiall Lightning in their Heavens.' Whereas Faustus himself treats the devils, Mephostophilis in particular, with a certain degree of *sang-froid*, it must be understood that his scepticism was not that of the Elizabethan audience. The Devil was still a real and frightful personage to the general mind.

Although the Devil was entertaining, then, he was at the same time fervently believed in as an actual person, a demon with a history, roaming the earth like a lion 'seeking whom he may devour' (see the Bible, 1 Peter 5:8). Faustus would have seemed almost incredibly foolhardy in mixing in such company. It is difficult for a modern audience to share this view, since active belief in a personal devil has waned considerably.

To us, then, the see-saw of Faustus's feelings seems, perhaps, the mark of a vacillating, weak man, rather than of one in anguish. Although it is crudely done, if we insist on judging by modern standards, Marlowe is attempting to depict the ebb and flow of consciousness—the way we tend to be perpetually tugged by conflicting motives and pressures. The see-saw is within, and it may help us to consider that the devil can be within also, sitting on the see-saw. It is said that Martin Luther threw an ink-well at the devil in his study: there was nothing there beyond the projection of his own inner thoughts. Just because we may no longer believe in the devil, there is no reason for us to disbelieve in evil.

The clock strikes

The ending of *Doctor Faustus* deserves special study. One way in which the power of Faustus's last speech may be measured is to try to substitute other words for the orginal and then note the effectiveness of Marlowe's choices. This is one speech where there is almost no difference whatever between A-text and B-text—obviously, it was found in production that Marlowe's own words burn through any attempt to meddle with them. They have the inevitability of all great poetry.

Here are some suggestions for 'altering' the text, so as eventually to appreciate better Faustus's last speech (V.2.143):

(a) Replace the third with the first person, for example:

Ah, now *I* have but one bare hour to live,
And then *I* must be damned perpetually.

What difference does this make? To the meaning, none at all; to the effect, a good deal. When Faustus calls himself 'Faustus' he stands outside himself, as it were, commenting dispassionately; this makes the switch to the first person, thirteen lines into the speech, extraordinarily dramatic: 'Oh, I'll leap up to my God: who pulls me down?' It is as if the feeling of longing suddenly burst through the controlling voice.

(b) Replace some words with others carrying a similar meaning, for example:

Now you have but a minimal time to spend. (line 144)

Notice how less effective this is than the simple words, 'one bare hour to live'. The stresses fall equally on *one, bare,* and *hour.* And the final word 'live' is much more accurate than 'spend'.

Or substitute for 'see, see, where Christ's blood streams in the firmament' (line 156):

'Observe where Christ's blood flows in the heavens.'

All of the life is robbed from Faustus's feverish line here. When he cries, 'See, see', the repetition is dramatic—he is pointing, he is involving the audience, eagerly, with great feeling. Also, 'streams' is much more powerful than 'flows', because of the rush of energy implied; and the three syllables of 'firmament' are necessary to make up the metre, ending on a stress (where 'heavens' would end the line on an unstressed syllable, giving a sense of release or drop in energy). Also 'firmament' rather rhymes and carries on the sound of 'streams' and so unifies the line.

(c) Look at a longer verse 'paragraph', for example lines 167–73:

You stars that reigned at my nativity,
Whose influence hath allotted death and hell,
Now draw up Faustus like a foggy mist

Into the entrails of yon labouring cloud,
That when you vomit forth into the air
My limbs may issue from your smoky mouths,
So that my soul may but ascend to heaven.

Now condense and paraphrase it, for instance:

You stars under which I was born,
Determining my fate, turn me now
Into rain, so that evaporating
I may enter heaven.

This may be clearer, but it is a long way from what Marlowe actually meant. 'Reigned' strongly states the power of the stars to dictate destiny; and 'allotted' is clearcut: one is either damned or saved, and this is the 'fate' Faustus is *specifically* talking about. Also when he uses words such as 'entrails', 'vomit' and 'smoky', he is using very strong, expressive words, containing vivid, if ugly images, which impress on us his sense of self-loathing at the same time as his longing to escape. Finally, Faustus says 'my soul', not 'I', and the difference is crucial. He knows he must die; but he is here longing for the salvation of his immortal part, his soul, for which he would suffer the physical ignominy 'entrails' and 'vomit' suggest. Much more could be done in a similar manner, both here and in the passage where Helen appears (V.1.97–116). It is an exercise well worth the trouble involved, as it sensitises the reader to Marlowe's tact and resourcefulness in the use of language and in the use of rhythm.

Arranging your material

Methodology

It would be foolish to try to say, definitively, how criticism should be written. A concept of 'pluralism' has to be accepted in relation to the dissenting voices which issue from critics who comment on any major work of literature. This is a concept which students sometimes find very difficult to accept, especially if they see how scientific disciplines can provide simple, clear-cut formulas for the solutions to problems. But it is no weakness in literary criticism for there to be more than one approach, one interpretation of a text; the student is *not* looking for some final, immutable answer: he is looking, instead, for a plausible reading, a commentary which serves to illuminate what may be obscure or (at least) indicate an awareness of the techniques that an author uses to make the organic, effective/affective work we call a piece of literature.

Granted, then, that there is no single 'authorised' method of literary criticism, we can still isolate a few basic preliminaries to any attempt. The following is meant as a guide only, to be used intelligently, and thus with scepticism. (Following a model doggedly is the road to mediocrity, so far as literary criticism is concerned; you must try to develop a personal style.)

Consider the genre to which the work belongs, and seek a reliable definition. *Doctor Faustus* is a tragedy, and Aristotle's definition (in the *Poetics*, Chapter 6) supplies the basic definition of tragedy. The task becomes, then, one of analysing *Doctor Faustus*, to estimate its quality in relation to the tragic mode. This is formalist criticism, analysis in terms of the elements Aristotle supplies as basic to the form: plot, character, themes, language, and theatrical features (the staging). Analysis is fundamental to formalist criticism, and the way to do it is to compile on separate sheets (or better still, index cards) notes on the plot, the characters, etc. These notes ought to relate to significant technical matters. As Aristotle first noted, a play has three parts: a beginning, a middle, and an end, each developing logically out of the other. Other critics have referred to this development as the 'tragic rhythm', from purpose (or the hero's initial drive towards ruin), through the central scenes of passion or suffering resulting from this drive, and into a phase of perception, where the full consequences of the tragic action become visible to the hero and to the audience. Expanding these three stages slightly to encompass the implications we may say that a plot includes: (i) exposition, establishing the opening situation; (ii) the tragic act; (iii) the developments which ensue; (iv) the crisis or turning-point; (v) the recognition scene; (vi) the catastrophe or reversal; (vii) the ending. The overall criterion with regard to plot is unity: the play ought to cohere as a single, almost inevitable narrative unit. (Where a sub-plot exists, it ought also to fit into the overall development in a subsidiary way.)

If we analyse *Doctor Faustus* we see that the exposition reveals the situation of a man so restless as to be willing to take some awful step to fulfil himself; the tragic act lies in the signing of the contract with Mephostophilis. So far, so good. But then we would have to recognise that the developments after this are episodic; they are rather too freely reliant upon spectacle and farcical material. The tragic rhythm is loosened here in the middle of the play (the student should find the details of this claim from the text of the play, Acts III and IV). In Act V the rhythm tightens again, and may be discussed in the above terms. You might ask yourself these questions: Is there a crisis towards the end of *Doctor Faustus*? Would you say, instead, that the turning-point comes early on? Is it not when Faustus makes the contract? If this is so, it is to remark the peculiar form of Marlowe's tragedy. Are you able to compare his structure with that of, say, *Hamlet* or *Macbeth*, where opposing characters may win the initiative?

When analysing characters, the student notes what they say, what they do, and what others say about them. And examining what others say about them is often the best way to begin, because the playwright may inform the audience in this way how to estimate the hero. In *Doctor Faustus* the Chorus tells us straight away what kind of man Faustus is; and then we hear Faustus himself describe his frustrations and aspirations. His friends, thirdly, offer some helpful comments on his intelligence and fame, and so we build up a composite picture from the text (*not* from surmise) of the nature of this particular tragic hero. Then we see him in action, and judge of his character by his relations with Mephostophilis. The moral question invariably enters characterisation of the tragic hero (as Aristotle said), only the man who is neither perfect nor villainous, but in between, is the proper subject for tragedy. We ask ourselves constantly, therefore, how right or how wrong Faustus is in what he is doing; and we attempt to understand his moral decline and ruin.

When discussing themes, the primary point to be borne in mind is that tragedy is 'a mimesis of sacrifice', in a phrase of the contemporary Canadian critic Northrop Frye*; it is the imitation of a sacrifice where there is a victim whose destruction somehow appeases the forces of justice, who are also the forces of terror. If this premise is kept in view, there is less chance that we shall begin by finding the hero simply blameworthy. The theme of 'the fall' from greatness is the basic tragic theme. It obviously implies that the hero has many positive qualities, and these must be searched out so as to comment fairly on the action. Other themes are best described in terms of the hero's motives—in Faustus's case, his aspiration, his ambition, his hunger, and so on. The themes are a way of describing the central, continuing patterns of the action, and also a way of making clear the hero's contribution to his own fate.

After *Doctor Faustus* has been analysed and criticised formalistically, language and theatrical features are the remaining elements, and these, of course, provide basic evidence on the form of the tragedy. Here we must beware of regarding a play like *Doctor Faustus* as a piece of realism.

In the end, it is the effect of a play as a whole that counts. Therefore, all the elements separated for easier discussion cohere into an organic, unified piece. In criticising *Doctor Fasutus*, the 'world' of experience it encompasses is the significant entity; language and everything else relate to the final effect the play as a whole registers.

Some general hints

(1) A play must be read and re-read before any useful criticism is attempted. It is in the re-reading that one is able to see how themes appear, how character develops or declines. There is no short cut to the hard work of study and revision.

*In *Anatomy of Criticism*, Athenaum, New York, 1966, p. 214.

(2) An essay in criticism must be an argument, either for or against the thesis proposed in the question. For example, if the question is: '*Doctor Faustus* basically enacts the corruption of the self through pride. Discuss', then an appropriate answer would need, in the end, to state clearly whether this proposition is valid or otherwise. To argue cogently on such a question, all aspects of the topic need to be taken into account. The italics in the question tell us that it refers to the play as a whole; and the student understands that he must, therefore, write upon the development of the action, and state whether or not he thinks that the play describes (basically) 'the corruption of the self through pride'. Then he must examine the terms used here. *Corruption*: does Faustus decline from good to bad? *of the self*: is the private tragedy the main one, or is the play somehow more concerned with politics or history—the public scene? *through pride*: is this the basic, primary, cause of Faustus's downfall? Is his fall mainly the result of a flaw within himself, and is this flaw pride? Here is the core of the question, in that last sentence; to deal with it adequately the student needs to refer closely to the text. There is very little value in simply replying, 'Yes, I think Faustus is very proud and ambitious and he causes his own downfall'. Your task is to show that it is true, by a case built up from evidence taken from the text. One quotation is insufficient: there must be assembled a fair case for prosecution or defence (whichever it is) and, accordingly, as many references as possible should be given—or combined quickly—in support of the case.

(3) An essay must be objective, not impressionistic. This point flows from the one just made. An argument, to be fair and logical, should employ its terms without prejudice. Criticism should avoid subjective appreciation, such as 'I think Faustus is a wonderful character, and he is very honest and brave and forthright'. This is just a personal view—of no value whatever, unless it is backed up all the way by reference to and quotation from the text. Then the way to proceed would be to take each adjective in turn: *honest, brave, forthright* and show how this is so. It would quickly be found that, even if true, this description is leaving out other qualities at least as (if not more) important, such as, say, *sceptical, curious, foolhardy* or *hedonistic*. The personal view is too vague to be of much use in criticism. The student should force himself to go beyond it, testing his ideas and refining them in the light of the text as a whole. All the time, he should ask himself, 'am I being fair to the text?' and then seek to phrase his thoughts accurately.

(4) As well as being an argument, and an objective description of the nature of the text, a piece of criticism is an exercise in persuasion. It is a question of trying to persuade a reader to accept a train of thought. Therefore, style (which here includes the tone of the writer, the language and the structure he uses) matters.

The tone should, in wisdom, be modest and unassuming; the writer should avoid imperatives, such as telling the reader, 'Note how Faustus forces Mephostophilis to answer his questions'. It is not up to the reader to 'note' anything; it is up to the writer to describe Faustus's situation in such a way that the reader clearly sees whatever he is supposed to see. The tone should also be as pleasant as possible, without being facetious or flippant.

The style should be clear and effective. This means, firstly, sentences free of grammatical errors, and secondly, a language free of jargon, clichés or meaningless phrases. Short sentences are preferable to long sentences. Adjectives should be used sparingly, and always with strict accuracy (a dictionary is an essential part of a writer's equipment). Vague phrases, even if used by newspapers, ought to be kept out. A bare, honest style is best.

At the same time, care should be taken with paragraphing, since the essay as a whole derives its effectiveness from its development. The wider aspect of style, then, is the structure of the essay as a whole. This will only be sound, and clear, if the writer has taken the trouble to make an outline first and has worked from that plan.

(5) 'Practice makes perfect,' the old proverb runs. Criticism, like every form of writing, is learned mainly by doing, and even more by re-doing, by re-writing. It is a complete illusion that writers sit down and dash off their thoughts (or stories) without the drudgery to which lesser mortals are subject. The best writers re-write and revise constantly, and the student would be foolish to imagine that he can master the craft of writing with less trouble than the best writers suffer. Obviously, under the conditions of a written examination re-writing is not feasible, except for partial re-writing; but this kind of test implies the discrimination of the practised student from the one who has left himself untrained: the former will be able to plan and organise and write an essay with greater skill and ease, even under pressure, than the student insufficiently practised. Therefore, an intelligent student should practise writing as much as possible, as a self-imposed discipline.

Some specimen questions

(1) Do you think that the lines of the Chorus which end *Doctor Faustus* sum up satisfactorily the meaning of the play?

(2) What significance do you attach to the congealing of Faustus's blood at the signing of the contract with Lucifer?

(3) Comment on the relation between the comic and the serious material (or plots) in *Doctor Faustus*.

(4) Write a critical analysis of the language used in Faustus's address to Helen, in V.1.97–116.

(5) What would you reply to the view that Faustus is essentially an arrogant egotist who deserves the fall to which his pride dooms him?

(6) In what way or ways would you say Faustus is a 'modern' man, whose ruin can be related to modern life?

(7) It has been said that Marlowe is primarily a poet and only secondarily a dramatist. What do you think is implied by this criticism, and do you agree with the implications?

(8) 'Doctor Faustus is not a tragedy at all; it is a straightforward morality play.' Discuss fully.

(9) How do you think the spectacular scenes, involving (a) the devils, and (b) Faustus's travels, were staged in Elizabethan times?

(10) 'Marlowe superbly humanises the waste always implicit in tragic failure.' Discuss fully, with reference to Doctor Faustus.

Some model answers

(1) *Do you think that the lines of the Chorus which end* Doctor Faustus *sum up satisfactorily the meaning of the play?*

[The student would, of course, need to be entirely familiar with the lines]
The lines of the Chorus are:

Cut is the branch that might have grown full straight,
And burned is Apollo's laurel bough,
That sometime grew within this learned man.
Faustus is gone. Regard his hellish fall,
Whose fiendful fortune may exhort the wise
Only to wonder at unlawful things,
Whose deepness doth entice such forward wits,
To practise more than heavenly power permits.

That these lines are meant to be summary, in the sense that they are spoken by the commentator who introduced the play at the beginning, appears to be obvious. The question remains whether this summary is of the 'meaning' of the play. A further question remains whether the summary—even if it can be shown to be of the 'meaning'—is 'satisfactory'. [*Here the attempt is to grapple with the terms of the question at the outset, and to make smooth the path for the following paragraphs.*]

What does the summary actually say? It says, in effect, that Faustus, who had much potential, is dead, and that his death should be a warning to others. The language used in the first three lines makes clear that the speaker found Faustus both admirable and reprehensible. He calls him 'learned', and admits that he had genius (for so the phrase 'Apollo's laurel bough', the badge of the inspired poet, may be interpreted). No one could question this view. From the outset of the play, Faustus appears to us as a man out of the ordinary, a scholar who, as his colleague puts it, 'was wont to make our schools ring with *sic probo*' (I.2.2). And the Chorus himself told us in his first address that Faustus excelled all of his contemporaries in scholarship (lines 16–18). Before ever he gained the advantage of aid from Mephostophilis, then, Faustus was recognised as a man of great learning. The Chorus also implies that Faustus wasted this gift, or allowed it to be destroyed; but the Chorus is careful not to state this directly, preferring to use the passive voice, 'Cut is the branch . . . burned is . . . [the] bough.' We can easily accept that the potential of Faustus has been cut off, where we might argue at some length over Faustus's own fault in this process.

The line, 'Faustus is gone. Regard his hellish fall', leads into the direct exhortation of the audience to see in Faustus's ending a moral, a warning. The choice of words is again unexceptionable. 'Gone' rather than 'damned' is tactful, for it preserves a sense of Faustus's humanity, his worth: why kick a man when he is down? Moreover, 'hellish fall' clarifies sufficiently where he is 'gone' to; so we do not find the Chorus being vindictive or superior here, and we attend the more readily to his final lines. They are somewhat vague, but to some purpose. Just as 'hellish' might be thought ambiguous (it can mean 'into hell' or 'a process in itself evil') so also 'fiendful fortune' retains just enough sympathy for Faustus as to keep our assent. It is as if the Chorus referred to 'devilish luck', either 'the fate suited to fiends', or 'a most unfortunate outcome'. Likewise, 'may exhort' where 'should' or 'must' could have been used, is supremely tactful. We are not being preached at too bluntly; and being included among 'the wise' makes our continuing assent easy. The last lines are tolerant enough to keep this assent. We are allowed to 'wonder at' what are vaguely termed 'unlawful things'; a more severe prohibition might have been expected. And there is the admission of admiration again in the phrase 'forward wits', referring obviously to Faustus; he is being regarded as reckless but not evil, for the 'deepness' of the forbidden area *entices* or attracts such natures. The last line, if it be taken as a generalisation of what Faustus has done, is as fair and generous as could be—he is not spoken of as having done evil to anyone but simply of having practised 'more' than is permitted: the emphasis is positive rather than negative, 'heavenly' (contrasting with 'hellish' above) makes 'power' seem benign, and the last word of all—'permits'—is open and is in the present tense, implying the order which governs speaker and audience in real life.

Thus, in tone and language the speech as a whole is one which avoids offence to the audience. It is humane and tolerant, and therefore civilised. There is no trouble in finding the speech both fair comment on Faustus's 'fall' and a reasonable explication of its moral implications. I would not be happy, however, with the description of the speech as a summary of the 'meaning' of the play, since this suggests that the play is simple where it is complex: surely it would not be possible to sum up a tragedy in eight lines? If it were possible, why should the playwright take the trouble to write some two thousand? What the speech summarises, I would maintain, is not so much the 'meaning' of the play as the significance of the hero's destruction; and because it offers this summary in a tactful and humane manner the speech in no way cuts across the tragic effect of the play itself. It does not interfere with the effect; but it controls the audience's response, as a Chorus necessarily does. This control ensures a coherent reception of the play, and for that reason it is 'satisfactory'. Indeed it is more than satisfactory. It is outstanding.

---

(5) *What would you reply to the view that Faustus is essentially an arrogant egotist who deserves the fall to which his pride dooms him?*

First of all, I would suggest that the terms of the question appear loaded. Anyone, any character, who could be described as an 'arrogant egotist' no doubt deserves some punitive treatment; but when we are told in addition that 'pride' somehow 'dooms him' then we can only feel that he 'deserves' it. With all respect, I must say that in relation to *Doctor Faustus* the questioner here seems to me to be begging the question.

But looking past this difficulty, one may see in the question several components which bear directly on the character and tragic fall of Faustus, and I shall attempt to examine these in detail. [*The purpose of these two paragraphs is to sift the wording of the question, so as to clear the decks for an answer that will not be vague or generalised. Care should be taken not to overdo this sifting; not to spend time quarrelling with the question when one should be answering it.*]

An egotist is one who concerns himself exclusively with personal interests. He is reprehensible on this account, since social relations depend upon the unselfishness (or at least the good will) of the members of that society. 'No man is an island,' wrote John Donne, and we acknowledge the truth of this claim; we are all members of some community whatever its political structure may be. 'Arrogant' means haughty or presumptuous. An 'arrogant' egotist implies a man who is aware that he is an egotist, or is anti-social, and does not care. He is indifferent to the claims of others, and deliberately, perhaps even violently, serves only his own desires. [*This paragraph is concerned with clarifying the first part of the question; the next paragraph will apply the terms to the play.*]

Is Faustus an arrogant egotist? Is he deliberately and violently anti-social? He is certainly arrogant, for we can see in the very first scene that he is presumptuous to the point of dismissing as insignificant the whole world of scholarship. This arrogance is seen most particularly in his treatment of 'divinity', or theology. First he says, 'When all is done Divinity is best' (I.1.37), but after little more than ten lines it is 'Divinity, adieu!' He rejects divinity without any full or serious investigation, and without giving what one could call satisfactory reasons. He simply says 'That's hard' or 'What doctrine call you this?' and then, on no other basis than personal dislike, dismisses the word of God easily. Pride is evidenced here also, and I would argue that pride is Faustus's major vice or flaw. In turning to the study of black magic, necromancy, he shows that his motive is power, and thus one can see that his pride is a craving to discard his human limitations and achieve, by whatever means, god-like powers. As he says:

> All things that move between the quiet poles
> Shall be at my command. Emperors and kings
> Are but obeyed in their several provinces.

> (I.1.55–7)

And again: 'A sound magician is a demi-god' (line 61).

There would appear to be no doubt, then, that arrogance, and its twin vice, pride, are the main flaws in Faustus's character. As the Chorus says, at the beginning, Faustus is 'swol'n with cunning of a self-conceit' (line 20). Faustus knows himself that this pride is sinful. After the contract has been signed and sealed he meditates: 'My heart's so hardened I cannot repent' (II.1.18)—such hardening of the heart, or denial of charity, is the direct consequence of pride. It is significant that pride was the fatal flaw in Lucifer also, which cost him heaven—as Mephostophilis tells Faustus: 'aspiring pride and insolence' was the crime 'For which God threw him from the face of heaven' (I.3.67–8). This tells us plainly that Faustus is of the devil's party. The pageant of the Seven Deadly Sins further confirms this, for Pride is the first to appear and be greeted by Faustus (II.1.116ff.). In so far as he rejects God out of pride Faustus is Satanic, and must, of necessity, end up in hell.

Therefore, in one sense, Faustus undoubtedly 'deserves' the end to which he comes. But whether he is an egotist who deserves to 'fall' is another matter altogether. The situation in which Faustus is placed is such that close social relationships are not an essential feature. He is a monk, a scholar, and a solitary. He has his friends, but they understand his absence from them to be the acceptable practice among scholars. Indeed, one of them excuses Faustus's despair at the end by saying it comes from too much study: 'He is not well with being over-solitary' (V.2.35). No rebuke is implied but, rather, sympathy. It would not be fair, then, to judge Faustus as one might a man in secular society, who ought to be involved in emotional ties with other people, men and women. In the context, in view of his scholastic situation, Faustus appears 'normal' enough; at least we hear of no criticisms from either friends or servants as to his egotism or anti-social demeanour. And at the end, his feelings for his friends, his concern that they should leave him lest they be involved in his final agony, speaks in his favour. There is nothing egotistic about Faustus at this point.

It could, however, be argued that Faustus's conduct after he obtains his magical powers is that of a vain and self-centred man. He travels; he satisfies his various appetites; he displays prickly sensitivity whenever his powers are cast in doubt (as by Benvolio), and he indulges in foolery with his inferiors, knowing that he must be the winner in any conflict between them. All of this conduct implies vanity, and egotism also, since Faustus shows none of the social conscience that was to distinguish, for instance, Goethe's hero, in the end.

Yet, it seems inadequate to claim that the egotism of which Faustus is guilty should entitle us to say that he 'deserves' what comes to him in the end. I think it must be repeated that his major fault is his pride, and this alone motivates his pact with Lucifer, which, in turn, both satisfies his lust for power and also, in time, destroys him. If he were an out-and-out egotist we should not find his fall moving, for we should be witnessing what we desired most, the downfall of a hateful being, a villain. But the fifth act of *Doctor Faustus* is so presented that our sympathies are all on Faustus's side, as he agonises and dreads the inevitable end. Mephostophilis confesses to having tempted Faustus in the first place, and 'robbed' him 'of eternal happiness' (V.2.99). The blame is spread outside Faustus, and we can view his fall as we would the destruction of a sacrificial victim. To say that Faustus 'deserves' his fall is true in part, since his pride surrenders him to Lucifer, but the play also suggests that his fall is pitiful. Perhaps we feel a double response: intellectually, we accept the justice of Faustus's ruin, but emotionally, we are drawn to pity his sufferings. Our response is probably diminished if we judge Faustus solely as a man of pride, and not also, simply, as a man.

Notes on answering Question 7: *It has been said that Marlowe is primarily a poet and only secondarily a dramatist. What do you think is implied by this criticism, and do you agree with the implications?*

This is a vital question: the student needs first of all to show that the structure of the play is open to criticism, firstly, because of the mixture of comedy/farce and tragedy, and secondly because of the concentration on a single character. Making clear that Marlowe was, in all likelihood, not the author of the farcical scenes, the student could argue that only the serious scenes interested him. The student could then proceed to show, by quotation and close reference to the text, that certain passages stand out as intensely moving and poetic. He should indicate an awareness why such passages are lyrical or beautiful or intense. And finally, he would have to venture an opinion whether Marlowe was able to dramatise situations credibly, able to get inside the skin of Faustus, as it were, or whether he failed to give an 'imitation of an action' and provided only isolated lyrical passages.

A note on the use of quotation: In the above model answers exact references were given for quotations. This is not necessary in a written examination. Close knowledge of the text is essential, however, as is the ability to quote freely in support of your argument. The serious parts of *Doctor Faustus*, especially Acts I and V (including the Choruses), should be so familiar as to allow the student to quote aptly.

Part 5

Suggestions for further reading

The text

Christopher Marlowe: The Complete Plays, edited by J. B. Steane, Penguin Books, Harmondsworth, 1969. This, the most convenient modern edition, is both authoritative and cheap. It is the edition used and quoted from throughout these notes.

Doctor Faustus, edited by John D. Jump, Methuen, London, 1962; Manchester University Press, 1976. This is part of the Revels Plays Series. It has a good introduction, useful notes, and contains in an appendix the chief passages from *The Historie of the Damnable Life, and Deserved Death of Doctor John Faustus*, which was Marlowe's principal source for his play. This edition is available in paperback.

Marlowe's Doctor Faustus 1604–1616 Parallel Texts Edited by W. W. Greg, Clarendon Press, Oxford, 1950. This is a scholarly edition by W. W. Greg, which not only discusses exhaustively the two different versions, the A-text and the B-text, but prints both, side by side, with notes.

Doctor Faustus, edited by Fredson Bowers in *The Complete Works of Christopher Marlowe*, Volume 2, Cambridge University Press, Cambridge, 1973. The 'Textual Introduction' argues that the B-text includes the 1602 additions.

Other works by Christopher Marlowe

The best introduction to Marlowe is the reading of his other plays. These are: *Dido, Queen of Carthage*, the two parts of *Tamburlaine the Great, The Jew of Malta, Edward the Second* and *The Massacre at Paris*. In particular, *Tamburlaine the Great, Part I* should be read in conjunction with *Doctor Faustus*. The Penguin edition of *The Complete Plays*, edited by J. B. Steane (cited above), makes this quite feasible.

Marlowe also translated from Latin Lucan's *Pharsalia*, Book I, and Ovid's *Elegiae*; these translations, together with his unfinished long poem, *Hero and Leander*, and his miscellaneous short poems, can be found in Fredson Bowers's edition of *The Complete Works*, Volume 2 (cited above).

General reading

BEVINGTON, D. M.: *From 'Mankind' to Marlowe*, Harvard University Press, Cambridge, Massachusetts, 1962. A study of the morality play tradition and its relevance to Marlowe's drama.

BRADBROOK, M. C.: *Themes and Conventions of Elizabethan Tragedy*, Cambridge University Press, Cambridge, 1935, 1969. An excellent book with which to approach the study of *Doctor Faustus*.

FARNHAM, WILLARD (ED.): *Twentieth Century Interpretations of Doctor Faustus: A Collection of Critical Essays*, Prentice-Hall, Englewood Cliffs, 1969. This is useful, but, as with all such collections, the student must be careful not to let others do his thinking for him.

FOAKES, R. A. AND R. T. RICKERT (EDS.): *Henslowe's Diary*, Cambridge University Press, Cambridge, 1961. A useful source book on the Elizabethan theatre.

HENDERSON, PHILIP: *Christopher Marlowe*, Harvester Press, Brighton, 2nd edition, 1974. A basic critical study-cum-biography.

LEECH, CLIFFORD (ED.): *Marlowe: A Collection of Critical Essays*, Prentice-Hall, Englewood Cliffs, 1964. Another useful volume: compare it with the volume edited by Farnham (cited above).

LEVIN, HARRY: *The Overreacher: A Study of Christopher Marlowe*, Harvard University Press, Cambridge, Massachusetts, 1952. A standard work of criticism.

NAGLER, A. M.: *Shakespeare's Stage*, Yale University Press, New Haven, 1958. An excellent account, in simple detail, of the Elizabethan stage.

STEANE, J. B.: *Marlowe: A Critical Study*, Cambridge University Press, Cambridge, 1964. An excellent, stimulating exploration of Marlowe's plays.

WILSON, F. P.: *Marlowe and the Early Shakespeare*, Clarendon Press, Oxford, 1953. A scholarly book, to be approached only after the student has completed considerable reading in the field.

WRAIGHT, A. D. AND VIRGINIA F. STERN: *In Search of Christopher Marlowe*. Macdonald, London, 1965. A well researched biography, with a good deal of background supplied, and copiously illustrated. An easy book to read, and quite stimulating. This is the ideal book with which to begin a study of Marlowe.

The author of these notes

Christopher Murray, a graduate of the National University of Ireland and Yale University, is a Lecturer in the Department of English at University College, Dublin. His publications include an edition of an Irish Restoration comedy, *St Stephen's Green*, by William Philips (1979), and a study of the Regency theatre, *Robert William Elliston, Manager* (1975). He acted as secretary and edited the *Newsletter* of the International Association for the Study of Anglo-Irish Literature (IASAIL) from 1973 to 1976; in 1977 he joined the executive board of *Irish University Review*, edited by Dr Maurice Harmon. He is guest editor of the Spring 1980 issue of that journal, devoted to Sean O'Casey.

York Notes: list of titles

CHINUA ACHEBE
A Man of the People
Arrow of God
Things Fall Apart

EDWARD ALBEE
Who's Afraid of Virginia Woolf?

ELECHI AMADI
The Concubine

ANONYMOUS
Beowulf
Everyman

JOHN ARDEN
Serjeant Musgrave's Dance

AYI KWEI ARMAH
The Beautyful Ones Are Not Yet Born

W. H. AUDEN
Selected Poems

JANE AUSTEN
Emma
Mansfield Park
Northanger Abbey
Persuasion
Pride and Prejudice
Sense and Sensibility

HONORÉ DE BALZAC
Le Père Goriot

SAMUEL BECKETT
Waiting for Godot

SAUL BELLOW
Henderson, The Rain King

ARNOLD BENNETT
Anna of the Five Towns

WILLIAM BLAKE
Songs of Innocence, Songs of Experience

ROBERT BOLT
A Man For All Seasons

ANNE BRONTË
The Tenant of Wildfell Hall

CHARLOTTE BRONTË
Jane Eyre

EMILY BRONTË
Wuthering Heights

ROBERT BROWNING
Men and Women

JOHN BUCHAN
The Thirty-Nine Steps

JOHN BUNYAN
The Pilgrim's Progress

BYRON
Selected Poems

ALBERT CAMUS
L'Etranger (The Outsider)

GEOFFREY CHAUCER
Prologue to the Canterbury Tales
The Clerk's Tale
The Franklin's Tale
The Knight's Tale
The Merchant's Tale
The Miller's Tale
The Nun's Priest's Tale
The Pardoner's Tale
The Wife of Bath's Tale
Troilus and Criseyde

ANTON CHEKOV
The Cherry Orchard

SAMUEL TAYLOR COLERIDGE
Selected Poems

WILKIE COLLINS
The Moonstone
The Woman in White

SIR ARTHUR CONAN DOYLE
The Hound of the Baskervilles

WILLIAM CONGREVE
The Way of the World

JOSEPH CONRAD
Heart of Darkness
Lord Jim
Nostromo
The Secret Agent
Victory
Youth and *Typhoon*

STEPHEN CRANE
The Red Badge of Courage

BRUCE DAWE
Selected Poems

WALTER DE LA MARE
Selected Poems

DANIEL DEFOE
A Journal of the Plague Year
Moll Flanders
Robinson Crusoe

CHARLES DICKENS
A Tale of Two Cities
Bleak House
David Copperfield
Dombey and Son
Great Expectations
Hard Times
Little Dorrit
Nicholas Nickleby
Oliver Twist
Our Mutual Friend
The Pickwick Papers

EMILY DICKINSON
Selected Poems

JOHN DONNE
Selected Poems

THEODORE DREISER
Sister Carrie

GEORGE ELIOT
Adam Bede
Middlemarch
Silas Marner
The Mill on the Floss

T. S. ELIOT
Four Quartets
Murder in the Cathedral
Selected Poems
The Cocktail Party
The Waste Land

J. G. FARRELL
The Siege of Krishnapur

GEORGE FARQUHAR
The Beaux Stratagem

WILLIAM FAULKNER
Absalom, Absalom!
As I Lay Dying
Go Down, Moses
The Sound and the Fury

HENRY FIELDING
Joseph Andrews
Tom Jones

F. SCOTT FITZGERALD
Tender is the Night
The Great Gatsby

E. M. FORSTER
A Passage to India
Howards End
ATHOL FUGARD
Selected Plays
JOHN GALSWORTHY
Strife
MRS GASKELL
North and South
WILLIAM GOLDING
Lord of the Flies
The Inheritors
The Spire
OLIVER GOLDSMITH
She Stoops to Conquer
The Vicar of Wakefield
ROBERT GRAVES
Goodbye to All That
GRAHAM GREENE
Brighton Rock
The Heart of the Matter
The Power and the Glory
THOMAS HARDY
Far from the Madding Crowd
Jude the Obscure
Selected Poems
Tess of the D'Urbervilles
The Mayor of Casterbridge
The Return of the Native
The Trumpet Major
The Woodlanders
Under the Greenwood Tree
L. P. HARTLEY
The Go-Between
The Shrimp and the Anemone
NATHANIEL HAWTHORNE
The Scarlet Letter
SEAMUS HEANEY
Selected Poems
JOSEPH HELLER
Catch-22
ERNEST HEMINGWAY
A Farewell to Arms
For Whom the Bell Tolls
The African Stories
The Old Man and the Sea
GEORGE HERBERT
Selected Poems
HERMANN HESSE
Steppenwolf
BARRY HINES
Kes
HOMER
The Iliad
The Odyssey
ANTHONY HOPE
The Prisoner of Zenda
GERARD MANLEY HOPKINS
Selected Poems
WILLIAM DEAN HOWELLS
The Rise of Silas Lapham
RICHARD HUGHES
A High Wind in Jamaica
THOMAS HUGHES
Tom Brown's Schooldays
ALDOUS HUXLEY
Brave New World
HENRIK IBSEN
A Doll's House
Ghosts
Hedda Gabler

HENRY JAMES
Daisy Miller
The Ambassadors
The Europeans
The Portrait of a Lady
The Turn of the Screw
Washington Square
SAMUEL JOHNSON
Rasselas
BEN JONSON
The Alchemist
Volpone
JAMES JOYCE
A Portrait of the Artist as a Young Man
Dubliners
JOHN KEATS
Selected Poems
RUDYARD KIPLING
Kim
D. H. LAWRENCE
Sons and Lovers
The Rainbow
Women in Love
CAMARA LAYE
L'Enfant Noir
HARPER LEE
To Kill a Mocking-Bird
LAURIE LEE
Cider with Rosie
THOMAS MANN
Tonio Kröger
CHRISTOPHER MARLOWE
Doctor Faustus
Edward II
ANDREW MARVELL
Selected Poems
W. SOMERSET MAUGHAM
Of Human Bondage
Selected Short Stories
GAVIN MAXWELL
Ring of Bright Water
J. MEADE FALKNER
Moonfleet
HERMAN MELVILLE
Billy Budd
Moby Dick
THOMAS MIDDLETON
Women Beware Women
THOMAS MIDDLETON *and* WILLIAM ROWLEY
The Changeling
ARTHUR MILLER
Death of a Salesman
The Crucible
JOHN MILTON
Paradise Lost I & II
Paradise Lost IV & IX
Selected Poems
V. S. NAIPAUL
A House for Mr Biswas
SEAN O'CASEY
Juno and the Paycock
The Shadow of a Gunman
GABRIEL OKARA
The Voice
EUGENE O'NEILL
Mourning Becomes Electra
GEORGE ORWELL
Animal Farm
Nineteen Eighty-four

JOHN OSBORNE
Look Back in Anger

WILFRED OWEN
Selected Poems

ALAN PATON
Cry, The Beloved Country

THOMAS LOVE PEACOCK
Nightmare Abbey and *Crotchet Castle*

HAROLD PINTER
The Birthday Party
The Caretaker

PLATO
The Republic

ALEXANDER POPE
Selected Poems

THOMAS PYNCHON
The Crying of Lot 49

SIR WALTER SCOTT
Ivanhoe
Quentin Durward
The Heart of Midlothian
Waverley

PETER SHAFFER
The Royal Hunt of the Sun

WILLIAM SHAKESPEARE
A Midsummer Night's Dream
Antony and Cleopatra
As You Like It
Coriolanus
Cymbeline
Hamlet
Henry IV Part I
Henry IV Part II
Henry V
Julius Caesar
King Lear
Love's Labour Lost
Macbeth
Measure for Measure
Much Ado About Nothing
Othello
Richard II
Richard III
Romeo and Juliet
Sonnets
The Merchant of Venice
The Taming of the Shrew
The Tempest
The Winter's Tale
Troilus and Cressida
Twelfth Night
The Two Gentlemen of Verona

GEORGE BERNARD SHAW
Androcles and the Lion
Arms and the Man
Caesar and Cleopatra
Candida
Major Barbara
Pygmalion
Saint Joan
The Devil's Disciple

MARY SHELLEY
Frankenstein

PERCY BYSSHE SHELLEY
Selected Poems

RICHARD BRINSLEY SHERIDAN
The School for Scandal
The Rivals

WOLE SOYINKA
The Lion and the Jewel
The Road
Three Shorts Plays

EDMUND SPENSER
The Faerie Queene (Book I)

JOHN STEINBECK
Of Mice and Men
The Grapes of Wrath
The Pearl

LAURENCE STERNE
A Sentimental Journey
Tristram Shandy

ROBERT LOUIS STEVENSON
Kidnapped
Treasure Island
Dr Jekyll and Mr Hyde

TOM STOPPARD
Professional Foul
Rosencrantz and Guildenstern are Dead

JONATHAN SWIFT
Gulliver's Travels

JOHN MILLINGTON SYNGE
The Playboy of the Western World

TENNYSON
Selected Poems

W. M. THACKERAY
Vanity Fair

DYLAN THOMAS
Under Milk Wood

EDWARD THOMAS
Selected Poems

FLORA THOMPSON
Lark Rise to Candleford

J. R. R. TOLKIEN
The Hobbit
The Lord of the Rings

CYRIL TOURNEUR
The Revenger's Tragedy

ANTHONY TROLLOPE
Barchester Towers

MARK TWAIN
Huckleberry Finn
Tom Sawyer

JOHN VANBRUGH
The Relapse

VIRGIL
The Aeneid

VOLTAIRE
Candide

EVELYN WAUGH
Decline and Fall
A Handful of Dust

JOHN WEBSTER
The Duchess of Malfi
The White Devil

H. G. WELLS
The History of Mr Polly
The Invisible Man
The War of the Worlds

ARNOLD WESKER
Chips with Everything
Roots

PATRICK WHITE
Voss

OSCAR WILDE
The Importance of Being Earnest

TENNESSEE WILLIAMS
The Glass Menagerie

VIRGINIA WOOLF
Mrs Dalloway
To the Lighthouse

WILLIAM WORDSWORTH
Selected Poems

WILLIAM WYCHERLEY
The Country Wife

W. B. YEATS
Selected Poems

York Handbooks: list of titles

YORK HANDBOOKS form a companion series to York Notes and are designed to meet the wider needs of students of English and related fields. Each volume is a compact study of a given subject area, written by an authority with experience in communicating the essential ideas to students of all levels.

AN INTRODUCTORY GUIDE TO ENGLISH LITERATURE
by MARTIN STEPHEN

PREPARING FOR EXAMINATIONS IN ENGLISH LITERATURE
by NEIL McEWAN

EFFECTIVE STUDYING
by STEVE ROBERTSON *and* DAVID SMITH

THE ENGLISH NOVEL
by IAN MILLIGAN

ENGLISH POETRY
by CLIVE T. PROBYN

DRAMA: PLAYS, THEATRE AND PERFORMANCE
by MARGERY MORGAN

AN INTRODUCTION TO LINGUISTICS
by LORETO TODD

STUDYING CHAUCER
by ELISABETH BREWER

STUDYING SHAKESPEARE
by MARTIN STEPHEN *and* PHILIP FRANKS

AN A·B·C OF SHAKESPEARE
by P. C. BAYLEY

STUDYING MILTON
by GEOFFREY M. RIDDEN

STUDYING CHARLES DICKENS
by K. J. FIELDING

STUDYING THOMAS HARDY
by LANCE ST JOHN BUTLER

STUDYING THE BRONTËS
by SHEILA SULLIVAN

STUDYING JAMES JOYCE
by HARRY BLAMIRES

ENGLISH LITERATURE FROM THE THIRD WORLD
by TREVOR JAMES

ENGLISH USAGE
by COLIN G. HEY

ENGLISH GRAMMAR
by LORETO TODD

STYLE IN ENGLISH PROSE
by NEIL McEWAN

AN INTRODUCTION TO LITERARY CRITICISM
by RICHARD DUTTON

A DICTIONARY OF LITERARY TERMS
by MARTIN GRAY

READING THE SCREEN
An Introduction to Film Studies
by JOHN IZOD